Recovering Truth, Freedom, and Democracy:
Challenging Woke Totalitarianism

Rev. John Gishler

Contents

Foreword

In *Going Spiritual: Discovering, Developing and Healing a Spiritual Life*, I shared how the supernatural dimension works. Here I am applying that knowledge, and my background in economic development, to update Nietzsche and Francis Schaeffer's warning that the loss of respect for the divine would lead to social chaos and the rise of totalitarian rulers. Freedom of speech and thriving democracy has only developed in countries where divine spiritual truth is respected in the culture. This is a guide to what has been lost and plan to recovering objective truth, freedom, and democracy by challenging woke totalitarianism.

Note to the Reader

All Bible quotations are from the *Holy Bible, New International Version* (Grand Rapids, Michigan: Zondervan, 2013), used with permission.

Introduction

Truth, freedom, and democracy are worth fighting for. Truth is the existential issue of our time. Truth is what has been seen to be true in many times and places by many people and cannot be disproven. Truth depends on the self-discipline and honesty of those who record and pass it down to later generations. This depends on there being real consequences for lying — the false witness of the Ninth Commandment. People who fear divine judgement if they deceive or fail to love their neighbour and have the hope of forgiveness in Jesus and eternal spiritual life are more likely to record and pass truth down reliably.

The cover drawing shows truth, freedom and democracy crumbling because the foundation of seven Judeo-Christian spiritual truths that all thriving Western democracies were built on is crumbling. These supernatural truths and values motivated people to love and trust their neighbour, fear divine judgement and gave them hope for forgiveness in Jesus and eternal spiritual life. Believers could work together, trust their neighbour and accept the rule of the majority. As we are seeing and Nietzsche predicted, the cultural loss of respect for divine truth has led to intolerable spiritual and social chaos, violence and the election of more totalitarian leaders in the U.S. and Europe.

This loss of respect for divine truth happened over centuries. The clergy became intellectualized, politicalized. They lost the guidance and healing power of the Holy Spirit that had authenticated their teaching. Pierre Burton's *"The Comfortable Pew"* criticized the Anglican bishops in Canada for failing to defend the Faith and challenge radical liberalism.

Postmodernism and the rise of wokeism accelerated the decline in the 1960s. The Oxford English Dictionary defines "woke" as:

Woke began as a call to African Americans in the United States to become more alert to "racial prejudice and discrimination."[1] An early example in the United States was the paramilitary youth organization, the Wide Awakes. They which formed in Hartford, Connecticut, in 1860 to support Abraham Lincoln the Republican candidate in the 1860 presidential election.

"Beginning in the 2010s, woke came to be used as slang for a broader awareness of social inequalities such as racial injustice, sexism, and denial of LGBTQ rights. Woke has also been used as shorthand for some ideas of the American Left involving identity politics and social justice, such as white privilege and reparations for slavery in the United States".[2,3,4,5]

Wokeism is a minority struggle for political and social power by activists who are often different, less qualified and morally and spiritually confused. It is a failure to take responsibility for a failed lifestyle or values and adapt to the more historically successful truths and values of Judeo-Christian cultures.

Life is competitive. The most fit succeed. Those who fear God are obligated to self-sacrificial love of neighbour and care for those who are less fit. Giving away 10% of your income to those in need is a serious test of love of neighbour. Wokeism attracts those who are trying to get ahead, without adopting the Judeo-Christian spiritual truths and values needed to thrive.

Wokeism is a child of Postmodern philosophy that is defined as:

> *"...of, relating to, or being a theory that involves a radical reappraisal of modern assumptions about culture, identity, history, or language"*[6]

Postmodernism rejects concepts of rationality, objectivity and universal truth. Instead, it emphasizes the diversity of human experience and multiplicity of perspectives."[7] Richard Wolin summarizes the conclusion of French philosopher Jean-Francois Lyotard's pioneering work on postmodernism as: "(there is no universal 'truth' or 'reason')"[8].

Postmodernism is an irrational, atheist way of thinking that is based on minority opinion without any over-arching sense of order. In simple language it seems to be the chaos of extreme liberalism gone mad in its rejection of historical experience, reason and divine authority and order.

Recovering the foundation of objective spiritual truth will lead to recovering objective truth in science. It will recover competition and excellence in education and business. Truth is the existential issue in our time of serious decline in academic test scores, political trust, identity confusion, disinformation and military aggression. We live in a nuclear armed world, and democracies are failing. Mette Frederiksen, Denmark's Social Democrat prime minister has called for a spiritual rearmament after realizing Danish men were not willing to join the army and fight for a socialist paradise. They need the motivation of something higher than human opinion.[9]

The good news is that the silent majority is tired of woke totalitarianism. The silent majority in the U.S. has revolted against Democratic Party wokeism and re-elected Donald Trump — warts and all, as Nietzsche warned. If you want more world leaders like Trump just do nothing. During his address to the Canadian parliament, President John F. Kennedy said, "As the great parliamentarian Edmund Burke said, 'The only thing necessary for the triumph of evil is for good men to do nothing.'"

The good news is that the silent majority is not doing nothing. New Christian churches are springing up that are teaching the objective spiritual truths of the Bible and thriving. A huge majority of voters in Ireland defeated their governing parties proposed woke agenda. Electric vehicles are piling up unsold in storage. Since 2023, 81 anti-DEI bills that target programs at U.S. colleges have been introduced in 28 states and in Congress. [10]

But this is just the beginning of the revolt against woke totalitarianism and spiritual and social chaos. Destructive woke false truths are deeply embedded in many churches, schools, universities and professional associations — and in law. This is a local challenge where each of us has some influence in our church, school, university or profession. We still get to vote for those who govern us and who fund schools and colleges.

To be effective in recovering truth, freedom and democracy the silent majority needs to understand:

1. The foundation of Judeo-Christian spiritual truth that underpins all free and thriving democracies (Chapter *1: The Lost Foundation of Spiritual Truth*, page 7);

2. How this foundation of truth was lost to the extreme liberalism, humanism and wokeism of human reason (Chapter *2: Human Reason as False Truth*, page 13);

3. The research that exposes liberalized Christianity, climate emergency, sexual identity confusion, diversity, equity and inclusion. as the opposite of the objective truth of the Bible, science, psychology and history (Chapters 3–8, pages 23–145); and

4. What you can do to recover objective truth, freedom and a democratic compromise that respects the rule of the majority and the needs of minorities (Chapters 9–11, pages 145 onward).

Truth, freedom, and democracy are worth fighting for!

1: The Lost Foundation of Spiritual Truth

"Shared beliefs simplify the world, as well, because people who know what to expect from one another can act together to tame the world." [11]

"The King James Bible was read in every church throughout the country (England) and the archaic language which was heard so regularly by so many embedded itself in the nation's conscience and vernacular". [12]

"Truth is a strong god that beckons us to the matrimony of ascent."

R. R. Reno, *Return of the Strong Gods: Nationalism, Populism, and the Future of the West*

In my first career as an economist, I was interested in why some countries developed politically and economically while others became failed states ruled by dictators. I discovered that real parliamentary democracy and the industrial revolution first began in England. The unique thing about England was that unlike Europe where corruption and wars of religion had discredited the Church; the Bible had been translated into English in 1611 and was the only book available to most people. It was deeply embedded in the culture.

Personal freedom and thriving democracy have been seen in all places and times to depend on a Judeo-Christian cultural foundation of shared truths. Citizens can trust each other to keep God's Commandments and resolve conflict by accepting the will of the majority.

The seven truths of the Judeo-Christian foundation of truth have been seen to be true in all places and times including our own. They are invisible spiritual truths.

They are the supernatural dimension working in the natural or physical dimension. The evidence of these truths proved the authenticity of Jesus and the Apostles and the Church He founded. Together they form a complete, coherent understanding of the relationship between the divine and mankind. If one is not seen to be true, Christianity becomes incoherent. For example, if Jesus was not the divine Son of God, He could not atone for the sins of the whole world, and we are all spiritually dead in our sin.

1.1: The Holiness of God

The holiness of God is the sum and essence of the foundation of the supernatural truths that bind us together under divine authority and judgement. The Ten Commandments are rules for life that define how we are to obey God and love our neighbour to be in a holy relationship with God and our neighbour. "Holy Matrimony," for example, is the spiritual opposite of same-sex marriage. God is not like us. God is the holy — pure, whole, complete, undivided, all-knowing, all-powerful creator of everything. We are unholy, impure, incomplete, divided, and unknowing. The central teaching of the Bible is that individuals who rebel against God's order, like Adam and Eve, are guilty of sin (rebellion), made unholy, and cannot be in God's holy presence in heaven when they die.

1.2: The Process and Order of Creation

The creation story teaches us the importance of Darwin's overlooked process of creation. Evolution and survival of the fittest is God's order or way of ensuring creation evolves to show more of God's glory. This is how things get better. The order of creation is from less complex and competent to more complex and competent. Humans are at the top and working together in obedience to God as stewards of creation. This is the opposite of our satanic woke diversity, inclusion and equity policies which discriminate against better, excellence and competence in rebellion against God's plan. This is survival of the less fit, the different and the deluded.

1.3: Male and Female Identity and Relationship

The Creation Story teaches us that man and woman are created to be signs of God's glory in the world. They are jointly responsible for the continuing stewardship of creation. The Bible, physiology and psychology teach us that they are spiritually, psychologically, and physiologically designed to be opposite, interdependent, and incomplete without the other. Pope John Paul II described the greatest sign of the glory of God as the union in self-sacrificial love of these two opposites. They are spiritually joined together in Holy Matrimony to continue God's creation of humanity.

1.4: How Satan and Spiritual Evil Works

The competition model in the Creation Story includes Satan who deceives Eve into disobeying God's clear instructions not to eat the fruit of the tree of the knowledge of good and evil. She says God told her she would die if she ate the apple. Satan said she would not die. Both statements are true. Eve, like us, would die spiritually and be put out of an eternal relationship with God. She would not die physically until old age. We have an enemy of our souls, with an army of evil spirits who try to tempt us, deceive us, destroy us spiritually and separate us from God.

1.5: Jesus Divinity, Resurrection, and Forgiveness

"If you forgive anyone's sins, their sins are forgiven; if you do not forgive them, they are not forgiven."

John 20:23

Many Christians have not been taught the foundational biblical and spiritual truth that the Holy Spirit or Spirit of God came over Mary and caused her to conceive Jesus. (Matthew 1.18) If they cannot understand and believe in this supernatural truth, then they cannot believe in the divinity of Jesus. If Jesus was merely a man; then He logically cannot give His life for the sins of the world, and we are all dead in our sins. This all depends on the divinity and resurrection of Jesus. The Resurrection of Jesus celebrated at Easter is God's divine yes to the New Covenant of Jesus. God would accept the sacrificial death of Jesus as full payment for all the sins confessed and taken to Jesus for forgiveness. Our part is to believe in Jesus and show this by repenting, confessing, and asking Him for forgiveness. The Resurrection is objective truth. The Risen Jesus was seen and touched by many people in different places. Many people in our time have spoken to Jesus in heaven and returned to earth. I have talked to one of them. The evidence is that the witnesses' lives were and still are dramatically changed.

1.6: Supernatural Healing and Deliverance Ministry

"The Spirit of the Lord is on me, because he has anointed me to proclaim good news to the poor. He has sent me to proclaim freedom for the prisoners and recovery of sight for the blind, to set the oppressed free, to proclaim the year of the Lord's favour."

Luke 4.18–19

Supernatural physical and spiritual healing and deliverance in Jesus Name is unique to Christianity. No other religion can point to the physical evidence of this healing prayer ministry in many places and times up to the present. The miracles were evidence of the authenticity of Jesus message. The ministry includes supernatural physical healing and deliverance from spiritual oppression, through the confession of sins, forgiveness in Jesus' name, and prayer. Specifically gifted and anointed ministers act as a holy pipe through which the Holy Spirit can come and heal. In Chapter *9: Recovering Objective Truth* (page 145) this is explained more fully for the many pastors, clergy and laypeople who are unfamiliar with this ministry.

1.7: Holy Spirit as the Continuing Presence of Jesus

"When the Advocate comes, whom I will send to you from the Father — the Spirit of truth who goes out from the Father—he will testify about me."

John 15.26

The Holy Spirit is the Spirit of Truth, revealing and helping us understand the teachings of Jesus and the Bible. As the continuing presence of Jesus, the Holy Spirit comes (when invited) to believers with an amazing outpouring of spiritual gifts. We experience the guidance of the Holy Spirit intuitively as our conscience. The gifts of the Holy Spirit include healing, words of wisdom, words of knowledge, faith, healing, miracles, prophecy, distinguishing between spirits and tongues. Paul explains that these gifts are given as the Spirit desires. They are not a sign of spiritual superiority to be used for personal gain but to build up the community of the Church. This is why different people have different gifts — and why we need to be together in a church community.

To recover these spiritual truths, we all need to understand how they fit together and depend on each other as a coherent social foundation of discipline for the development and sustaining of freedom and democracy.

2: Human Reason as False Truth

"...the existence of a transcendent, all-powerful deity—had been fatally challenged. Nietzsche concluded from this that everything would soon fall apart, in a manner catastrophic both psychologically and socially."[13]

Jordan Peterson, *Beyond Order*[14]

Human reason as false truth is what we have been left with after centuries of deconstructing the Judeo-Christian foundation of spiritual truths on which our progressive Western freedom, democracy, was built. The loss of the Judeo-Christian foundation of truth and its replacement by human reason has led to "things falling apart," as Nietzsche predicted. The word "human" means weak, vulnerable, and fallible. This applies particularly to our thinking which is built on assumptions —some of which are likely to be wrong. I try to remember the parts of the word as "ass-u-me," or likely to make an ass out of you and me. Simple physical and emotional things like tiredness, sickness or trauma in our lives affect our ability to reason and know what is true and what is false. Many people have psychological needs and disorders which affect their thinking. We will examine the four critically flawed assumptions of human reason:

1. No foundation of objective spiritual truths

2. No Satanic deception

3. No psychological self-deception

4. No political motivation.

To recover the foundation of Judeo-Christian spiritual truth, we must understand how the key building blocks of objective spiritual truth were historically challenged and deconstructed by intellectualized clergy, liberal thinking, humanist philosophers, and modern woke activists. This will enable us to challenge the false truths of woke extremists, end the social chaos, and recover our freedom and democracy.

2.1: No Foundation of Objective Spiritual Truth

Francis Schaeffer's *How Should We Then Live?*[15] was a sweeping review of the rise and decline in Western art, architecture, music, and philosophy as the Judeo-Christian foundation of spiritual truth was built and then deconstructed. He explains how these spiritual truths, which motivated people to trust and work together in developing Western progressive culture, were gradually questioned, and lost.

More intellectual, liberal, and politicized clergy, who had not experienced the Holy Spirit; replaced these truths of the Bible with first the secular intellectual truth of humanism and reason, and now with woke minority opinion as truth in our post-truth culture.

> *By the Middle Ages, AD 500–1400, "...there was an ever-growing emphasis on salvation resting on man's meriting the merit of Christ, instead of resting on Christ's merit alone."*[16]

This sentence might give you a headache! It is sheer intellectualism. It bent backward the clear teaching of the Bible that each person can only depend on the grace of our Lord Jesus Christ for salvation; to imply we can earn that merit. And who determines how we earn the merit of Christ? - the Church. This was a religious power grab. Just do what the priest says. By the end of the Middle Ages, the great teacher, Thomas Aquinas "...began opening the door to placing revelation and human reason on an equal footing."[17] Aquinas, a leading theologian at the University of Paris, also began to deviate further from the divine truth of the Bible by teaching that when man (including woman) revolted against God, only the will had fallen, not the intellect. Makes you dizzy.

This paved the way for the next step, which was that "...philosophy was gradually separated from revelation — from the Bible, philosophers began to act in an increasingly independent autonomous manner." [18] They were free to go back to Aristotle (banned by Pope Urban) and mix pre-Christian philosophy with Christian philosophy. Schaeffer shows this change in philosophy in a painting by Raphael in the Vatican. The painting shows Plato pointing upward to the spiritual, together with Aristotle pointing downward to the particulars of life, as the source of meaning and purpose. Petrarch was the first in a line of professional humanist philosophers who venerated everything ancient including Greek and Roman thought, excluding early Christianity. This devalued, intellectualized, and eviscerated the supernatural cultural foundation of the Bible on which our modern democracy and economic progress rests.

The Protestant Reformation was a reaffirmation of the truth and authority of the Bible and its supernatural worldview and authority in determining truth. It happened in Europe and Great Britain, as faithful Christian teachers challenged the authority of the (Roman Catholic) Church to re-interpret and change the clear teachings of the Bible.

John Hus (1368–1415), at the University of Prague, was betrayed and burned as a heretic by the Catholic Church. Martin Luther's "95 Theses," or questions for discussion in 1517, also led to a charge of heresy.

Friends hid him in a castle for three years while he completed the first translation of the Bible from Hebrew and Greek into German.

In England freedom and democracy can be traced back to 1215 when a group of 40 barons forced King John to sign the Magna Carta (1215) guaranteeing freedom of speech and trial by jury. Wycliffe translated the bible from the Latin Vulgate to English in 1382–95. But it was the King James Version, translated directly from the original Hebrew and Greek in 1611, that was popularized and formed the truths of English culture. This preserved and embedded the Judeo-Christian foundation of spiritual truth in the culture and led to the unique Christian social order and economic progress of England. England had the first constitutional monarchy, first democratic parliament and first Industrial Revolution.

In contrast, the Enlightenment in 17th Century Europe challenged the supernatural authenticity of the Bible. Mathematician and philosopher Rene Descartes "solved" the philosophical problem of trying to apply reason to study the supernatural, intuitive, mystical dimension by dividing philosophy into two categories — and focusing on the physical category:

- *res cogitans* (a thinking something that has no spatial extension); and

- *res extensa* (a spatial something that has no psychic qualities}.[19]

Cartesian Dualism elevated (generally male) rational deductive thinking over (generally female) intuitive mystical spiritual thinking. This resulted in devaluation of the intuitive/mystical/personal experience-based spiritual truth of the Judeo-Christian foundation on which our progressive freedoms and democracy are based. This male rational thinking, separated from the feminine intuitive thinking, is the root cause of our Western social chaos and political decline. It is also why many countries that have lost or do not have this foundation of Judeo-Christian supernatural values — like Afghanistan, China, Pakistan, and Russia — have lost or failed to develop freedom of speech and thriving democracies.

In contrast to England, which had this Biblical foundation of values, Europe was plunged into long and destructive wars over Religion. The Foundation of spiritual truths and values was weakened. The result was increasing social chaos that led to revolutions in France and Russia, followed by destructive dictatorships and two world wars — as Nietzsche foresaw.

This loss of the divine foundation of spiritual truth of the Bible is the greatest flaw in human reason as an authority for truth. It was the glue that held people together in Western culture. People were motivated to fear divine judgement, love God and their neighbour with the self-sacrificial love of Jesus, and the hope of eternal spiritual life.

2.2: No Satanic Deception

The reality of Satan and spiritual evil is the second fatal flaw in depending on the authority of human reason in determining truth. Everyone has trouble really believing in the supernatural worldview of the Bible — until they experience it personally. We can affirm this supernatural reality, but it is very hard to really grasp. In my case I had gone through a divorce and decided to read the Bible. Reading the Bible naturally leads to praying the Bible. Prayer leads to experiencing the supernatural in the Bible and deeper faith. I began to gradually notice the Holy Spirit and experience the

Holy Spirit. Then I discovered the reality of Satan and deception. I was standing on a busy street corner in downtown Calgary; beside the woman I had just fallen in love with. As we waited for the light to change, I was noticing the huge volume of cars and trucks rushing past us in the traffic chaos known as rush hour. A thought quietly formed in my mind. "You could just push her a little and she would fall into the traffic and be killed, and nobody would know." I broke out in a cold sweat. I was stunned. Where the hell was this coming from! How could I hurt the woman I loved? Then the truth dawned like a bright light. This was from hell. We are not alone! Satan, who the Bible teaches was the angel of light before he rebelled against God and was cast out of Heaven to the earth, really does try to deceive people by whispering lies in their ears! This was one of my most dramatic and profound learning experiences.

Many people confuse evil with badness. They are very different. Evil is bad, but bad things can happen to people due to luck, nature, or poor judgement. Evil is "live" spelled backwards. Evil is personal and specifically destructive of spiritual life, with no benefit to anyone or anything. Evil is gratuitous destruction of human spiritual lives — Satan's payback to God for his banishment.

Satan is real. We ignore spiritual evil at our peril. Notice that all the woke false truths are destructive with no real gain and separate people from the divine and each other.

2.3: No Self-deception

Human reason naively assumes a level playing field. Human reason assumes our mind is neutral in analyzing information. This is a very dangerous assumption. It is not reasonable to assume our brains could bring to our attention every bit of information coming in from our physical senses — my finger is not hurting; my foot hurts; it is cold; there is a wind; I smell smoke; I see a car; etc. It would be overwhelming, and our mind would crash like a computer trying to find the square root of minus one. So, logically, there must be a filter to protect the mind from irrelevant information. The filter must have basic criteria for what is important and what is not. I was unaware of this as the following story revealed.

Psychology teaches us that our minds can suppress, distort, and hide vital information from us. This was a stunning discovery for me. It was based on reading the psychological works of Freud, Jung, and Goleman. Freud had begun helping people who were considered mentally weak. They were often suicidal, hysterical, spoke gibberish or were dysfunctional due to depression. They were an embarrassment to families and sent to asylums where they could be cared for until they either recovered or died. Freud developed what he called the "Talking Therapy." He listened until he could decipher the mumbling and gibberish into words and sentences. By persisting in questioning and listening, gradually Freud was able to help them recall the traumatic event or situation that had caused their condition. The traumatic memory had apparently been blotted out of their conscious memory. As they were able to recall and talk about the traumatic memory, their minds gradually healed.

Freud, the devout Jew, was doing almost the same work as a Christian priest. He was hearing a confession, assuring forgiveness, recovery, and releasing people from the emotional or spiritual bondage to the trauma. He was acting as a "soul doctor." "Freud changed the whole concept of mental illness by showing it was not the result of a weakness of intellect or a malfunction of the brain, but the impact of intense emotions on mental functioning."[20]

He reached another revolutionary conclusion, that the blocking out of an unpleasant idea from consciousness is an essential cause of hysteria, or what psychologists call neurosis.

Freud's most basic discovery was the existence of the subconscious as a separate part of the mind. Not only was there an unconscious part, but the unconscious part was also much bigger and more powerful than the conscious part.[21] His key discovery was that the unconscious part of the mind is very vulnerable to deception. Powerful emotions seem to be able to override our normal logical thinking.

> *"Finally, he realized that the unconscious part of the mind lacked a sense of reality. It did not distinguish between truth and emotionally charged fiction. That was the greatest secret."*[22]

Daniel Goleman, the bestselling author on emotional intelligence, wrote *Vital Lies, Simple Truths: The Psychology of Self-deception* in 1985. It was for me the right book at the right time. Goleman worked with patients "…whose very disorders seemed to protect them from some deeper threat."[23] This was like Freud, who discovered that repressing memories of traumatic events (often experiences of sexual abuse) had overloaded their minds and made them dysfunctional. Goleman also realized that self-deception is a by-product of a mental process that protects us from emotionally threatening or traumatic information. What comes to our conscious mind "…is a delicate balance between vigilance and inattention."[24] This is how he explained our ability to both know but not know at the same time.

Goleman developed a synthesis of neurology and psychology to explain the difference between the logical and the emotional parts of the human brain. Our brains have two separate paths for information. These paths developed as the primitive human brain evolved from dealing with simple fight or flight survival reactions (the emotions), to the much later logical part, which can do a much more complex analysis of situations. His point is that we need both. The emotional information adds emotional and spiritual information that enriches the higher logical analysis, so we make better decisions. We need the male rational working with the female intuitive spiritual mystical to find the best and deepest truths.

2.4: No Political Motivation

The last fatal flaw in reason is the naive assumption that human reason is not flawed by political motivation. The descent from objective truth to an opinion-based, post-truth culture is a complete break from the Judeo-Christian foundation of truth and values — including honesty

The assumption of political neutrality is simply a delusion that human beings can be neutral. The evidence is all around us. We will see how this has played out in the development of the false truths in the chapters that follow.

Chapter 3: *Liberalism as False Christianity*, exposes the naïve liberal activists who challenged biblical teachings on sin, salvation, Jesus, sexuality, marriage, and forgiveness, to create a new religion of liberalism that is the opposite of Judeo-Christian truth.

Chapter 4: *Climate Emergency as False Science*, exposes how New Left Marxist activists developed word manipulation tactics that confused the public and helped opportunistic socialist politicians, environmentalists and the ineffective wind and solar industries to waste billions of dollars, destroy the German energy market, double the cost of energy, and increase CO_2 emissions.

Chapter 5: *Feminism as False Female*, exposes the social confusion and psychological cost of women losing their unique identity and value in society. We will learn how the women's liberation movement was hijacked by a minority of extreme feminists who changed the original feminist goal of political equality with men, to "sameness as men" in applying for jobs.

The politicalization of male and female identity is exposed in Chapter 6. *Homosexuality as False Male.*

Chapter 7: *Diversity, Equity, and Inclusion as False Justice*, exposes New Left Marxist politicalization of economic truth to impose anti-capitalist stealth socialism.

Democracy is in decline around the world and dictatorships are growing stronger. Swiss philosopher and theologian, Francis Schaeffer, warned, "No totalitarian authority nor authoritarian state can tolerate those who have an absolute by which to judge that state and its actions."[25] The good news is that absolute truth works both ways. If dictators cannot tolerate those who have absolute truth; the way forward is to recover those absolute truths and use them to challenge woke false truths wherever we find them. We must support political actors who will oppose them in governing bodies. We all get to vote for those who lead our church, professions, universities, schools, and public boards. Let us keep it that way.

3: Liberalism as False Christianity

The extreme liberal deconstruction of the Bible and its Judaeo-Christian foundation of transcendent truth is the root cause of our confused post-truth culture and its descent into social chaos. The replacement of transcendent truth with truth of reason is driving our loss of objective truth, freedom, and democracy. We have already seen the consequences of this social chaos as people turn to dangerous but strong leaders (like Trump). This pattern was explained by Francis Schaeffer in *How Shall We Then Live?*[26] He gives the examples of social and political chaos in France leading to Napoleon, and chaos in Germany leading to Hitler.

Liberal philosophy naturally questions authority and tries to liberate individuals from anything that limits or controls their personal freedom — particularly political and religious freedom. In *Chapter 2: Human Reason as False Truth,* we traced the deconstruction of the ancient Judeo-Christian foundation of transcendent truth. We saw how the historic faith of the Hebrews and first Christian Apostles was gradually liberalized and changed. It began as a personal spiritual relationship and experience of God the Father, Jesus and the Holy Spirit in a small Holy Spirit-led community. This grew into an intellectualized and politicalized state religion as Christianity grew and expanded beyond the Roman empire.

Christianity was born as the followers of Jesus Christ, who had heard Him and seen divine healings, were rejected by the Jewish leaders, and put out of synagogues. Jesus was crucified for blasphemy — falsely claiming to be the Messiah. There had been many false Jewish prophets claiming divine authority. Jesus was the only one who had demonstrated supernatural healing power all over Israel. He healed people physically and spiritually and cast out demons. People knew intuitively His teachings were authentic.

The Jewish religious leaders who had not seen or experienced the supernatural themselves, could not believe Jesus was authentic. Sadly, the Pharisees and Teachers of the Law failed to see the consistency between the biblical prophecies about a saviour and teacher like Moses.

The Bible (Old Testament) was probably first written down from the ancient oral tradition during the Babylonian Captivity (586–538 BC). The New Testament books can be traced back to the letters of Paul in the second half of the first Century. The Gospel of John is probably the last written in its present form around 210 AD. Many people notice John is different and more powerful. This is because John and Mary the mother of Jesus both lived in Ephesus. It is an eyewitness account of the life of Jesus.

The historic liberal deconstruction of the Bible and the dismissal of its supernatural worldview as mythical has left us with a new religion of Liberalism, that is the opposite of biblical Christianity. Projected to its most extreme form, this new religion of liberalism has no concept of God being holy. It presents no theology of sin and redemption, no love for or fear of God, nor fear of divine judgement. Neither is there any concept of Satan or demonic influence to tempt and oppress people. There is no Holy Spirit to be the continuing presence of Jesus as guide, healer, and comforter. Projected to its extreme logical conclusion, what is left is a religion of works, where kindness and good works earn merit and reward, and possibly eternal life. Bad behaviour may be automatically forgiven by an unholy god of love. Jesus has been vaguely rebranded as a non-divine, good man and teacher who couldn't and didn't die for the imaginary sins of the world, because God just forgives everyone automatically. Yes, it is incoherent when projected to its extreme form. This is why we now have social chaos.

The liberalism I use here is an extreme teaching example of where many churches seem to be headed in our time. Liberalism is technically a mental stronghold. A mental stronghold is a psychological and spiritual delusion that cannot be reasoned with. Alcoholism is the most common example of a mental stronghold. We can build mental strongholds in our mind through a repeated pattern of sin. This gives Satan a "supernatural right" to oppress us. This reinforces the natural psychological process of self-deception, which blocks information that challenges what we believe from reaching our conscious mind. The late John L. Sandford commented that "all the 'isms' are mental strongholds." These are the spiritual "prisons" Jesus came to free people from.

To understand why Liberalism is a false form of Christianity, we will go through the Apostles' Creed, a basic statement of Christian Faith. This will show the theological differences between the Judeo-Christian faith of the Bible and where the alternative modern beliefs of woke liberal Christianity are leading. My reference for this comparison is J. Gresham Machen's *Christianity and Liberalism*. Machen very helpfully projects liberalism's attacks on Christian doctrine to their logical theological extreme. Machen was a preacher, as well as a Professor of New Testament Theology at Princeton. He appreciated the teaching value of extreme examples. This will help us understand what modern religious liberalism may not say clearly, but where, what it does say is headed theologically. It is headed to being a very different religion and false Christianity.

3.1: "I believe in God the Father almighty,
creator of heaven and earth."

The essence of God is His uniqueness, holiness, otherness, and un-knowableness. God is holy — pure, undivided, and whole. The unique thing about God the Father in the Bible is that He has acted and continues to act in history. God is not a principle, ideal, or just an object of worship. God is a person, a spiritual presence, our Father, who is almighty or all powerful, and has created everything in heaven and earth.

God is our spiritual Father. This is the first, most beautiful and most important thing the Apostles' Creed tells us about God. God loves us as a father loves each of us as his child. We do not have to be good to earn that love. It is always there no matter what we do.

The holiness of God is what I call God's dilemma. God the father loves us and desires a personal love relationship with each person. For someone to love God truly, they must be given the freedom to choose to not love and not obey God. The story of Adam and Eve in Creation illustrates exactly how this works. They are in a perfect obedient love relationship with God. They have everything they need — with only one limitation. They are to obey God's rule to not eat the apples from the tree of the knowledge of good and evil.

Satan, the snake, deceives them with the half-truth, "you will not certainly die" (Genesis 3:4). They disobey God and eat the forbidden fruit of the tree. They do not die physically, but their holy love relationship with God does die (spiritual death). They are put out of the Garden of Eden (i.e., heaven) for a temporary physical life of hard work and pain. The rest of the Bible is about God reaching out to people through prophets to bring them into a holy and obedient love relationship.

This is the opposite of liberalism which tries to liberate people from authority, rules, and tradition. Liberal Christianity, like the other woke false truths, sounds good at first but on closer examination is the opposite of Biblical Christianity. Extreme liberalism generally dismisses the whole Old Testament as superstition and myth. This is just self-deception. Some of the stories are wisdom stories, like Jesus saying, "There was a man..." The truth of these stories is deeper and more profound than the facts of history. The evidence of history supports the Old Testament as an accurate historical account. The Flood of Noah's time is recorded in ancient manuscripts, visible in geographical evidence and the remains of the ark are buried in ice in Turkey. There is physical evidence of the Exodus in Egypt and the conquest of Palestine by Joshua (1250 BC).

3.2: "…Jesus conceived by the power of the Holy Spirit and born of the Virgin Mary."

Many people believe in Jesus as a historical person — but they may believe in very different things about Jesus. The question is, what is it about Jesus that you believe in? What is it that you trust in? We begin with the most controversial issue in Christianity — the divinity of Jesus. This is one of our seven lost spiritual truths. If Jesus was not divine, then He could not die for the sins of the world, and we have no hope of eternal spiritual life with our holy God.

The Bible is very clear that Jesus proved He was the long-expected Messiah and only biological Son of God via the Holy Spirit. We are sons and daughters by adoption through faith. His work and miracles of healing, "opening the eyes of the blind" and "setting captives free," was prophesied by Isaiah over 500 years before Christ's birth (Isiah 61:1–3).

Who was the father of Jesus? If you answered Joseph, you need to read Matthew 1:1–22 and Luke 1:26–38. The correct answer is the Holy Spirit. This misunderstanding is why many Christians have trouble with honouring the Virgin Mary. I have heard many liberal academics foolishly arguing that "virgin" just means young girl. If you read the whole Bible, you get a very clear picture that Joseph being the real father is contrary to the evidence. The most dramatic evidence is the cute little story where Mary rides a donkey 90 km to Bethlehem. Think about it! Ask anyone who has been nine months pregnant if Mary would risk her life bumping along on a donkey for 90 km to be with her husband. Joseph could complete a census form without her. Mary was desperate! If she had stayed at home, the relatives probably would have killed her for being pregnant out of wedlock.

Then there is the curious matter of the inn being full. This is a public inn in a part of the world and time when welcoming a stranger is a religious obligation. Unless, of course, the relatives had gotten word out that they were not married. Mary was incredibly brave. She continues to be honoured in Christian churches as the perfect example of an awesome, faithful, humble, and obedient Christian woman. Visitors to Ephesus in Turkey still go to the house where she lived under John's protection as Bishop. Her eye-witness accounts of Jesus are in John's Gospel — which is the glory of Christianity.

Liberalism has disregarded and deconstructed this key supernatural teaching as mythical and superstitious. For many extremely liberal Christians, Jesus has been reduced to a non-divine man, who could not die for the sins of the world but was a wonderful teacher and example of good human moral behaviour. This is the exact opposite of what the Bible and Christianity teach. Liberalism has done great damage to the faith of many Christians and robbed them of the hope and lifegiving freedom of real forgiveness. This is one of the seven spiritual truths that needs to be recovered and taught in churches as the first step in recovering the foundation of spiritual truth our freedom and democracy rests on.

3.3: "He suffered under Pontius Pilate, was crucified, died, and was buried."

This statement is a response to ancient debates about whether Jesus was fully human, as well as fully divine. Some argued Jesus was not fully human and only appeared to suffer and die — for the sins of believers. This is a summary of historical fact as recorded in the Bible (Matthew 27:11–66; Mark 1:1–45; Luke 23:1–56; John 19:1–42). The Resurrection proved Jesus' death was divinely approved as sufficient to pay for the sins of the whole world. This is the essence of the New Covenant of Jesus. If you cannot believe this it may be time to read the Bible, be humble, surrender, invite the Holy Spirit into your life and come home.

Extreme liberals have trouble with the sacrificial death and resurrection of Jesus. They try to deny the resurrection with the delusion that maybe Jesus was just in a coma, didn't die and only appeared to be resurrected by God. This statement was included to refute the heresy of Docetism — that Jesus never had a fully human body and could not suffer and die physically. Read the eyewitness accounts in the Bible -- and watch the movie *The Passion of the Christ* — if you have the stomach. Nobody could survive crucifixion.

3.4: "On the third day He rose again. He
ascended into heaven and is seated at the
right hand of the Father."

This is the pivotal event in Christianity. The Biblical accounts sound authentic as they reveal the natural human confusion and weakness of the disciples (Matthew 27.62–28.20; Mark 16:1–8; Luke 24:1–53; John 20:1–25). If it was made up, there would be a very different story of angels, light, magnificence, and wise adoring disciples. The consistency of the Bible in describing the appearances of Jesus after the Resurrection is also very human and natural.

The best proof of the Resurrection is the changed lives of the Disciples, who went from being uneducated, confused fishermen, to becoming international evangelists, willing to die for their belief in the Resurrection. In our time there are still accounts in Africa of people being raised from death through Christian prayer ministry.

The descriptions of Jesus' Resurrection body indicate it could be both material and immaterial. He could move through locked doors, but could also eat, drink and be touched. The Ascension is consistent with the reality of the supernatural heavenly realm connecting to the earthly realm. Many people in our time have had visions of heaven with vast multitudes of joyful people praising God and basking in His presence. Others have had near death experiences (see the "Howard Storm" videos on YouTube) and talked to the Risen Jesus. Jesus is seated at the right hand of God and will be our Lord, brother, advocate, and judge when we arrive.

Extreme liberalism struggles with belief in the Resurrection, the Ascension, final judgement, and eternal spiritual life in heaven. These beliefs are all dependent on the authenticity of the supernatural dimension of the Bible that extreme liberalism dismisses as mythical and superstition. Once you start to deconstruct the supernatural in the Bible as mythical, superstitious, and not true; you end up with the false Christianity of liberalism that only appears to be Christianity. Liberal Christians want the comfort of being Christian without the personal limitations. This is a delusion. Anyone who believes you only get what you can see will sadly get what they want.

3.5: "He will come again to judge"

Christians look forward to the second coming of Jesus. In our darkest hours we pray come quickly, Lord Jesus. We are end-time people because we believe the world is going somewhere, and that somewhere is the return of Jesus, and the establishment of His kingdom on Earth (Matthew 16:28; Revelation 1:7). There are many ways of interpreting this. The Jews (and Jesus was a Jew) had always looked forward to the last days. Jesus was often asked for the signs of when this will come (Matthew 24:1–51). His answer in Matthew has been the source of a whole end-times publishing industry, as various writers try to establish when this will be. For example, the clue Jesus gives in Matthew is, "So when you see standing in the holy place [the temple mountain] 'the abomination which causes desolation,' spoken of through the prophet Daniel — let the reader understand — then those who are in Judea flee to the Mountains" (Matthew 24:15–16). Assuming the abomination is the idol Baal, as symbolized by the horns of a cow or crescent moon, this could be the mosque built on the temple mountain with this symbol on top. Other theories have calculated from the establishment of the State of Israel in 1950 and projected forward the "seventy sevens" or 490 years in the Bible. (Daniel 9.25–27)

As I write, the prophesied Gog and Magog (Iran and Russia) are allies in a war with Ukraine and Iran has sponsored the current war against Israel. (Revelation 20.7–9) Someone has noticed the colours of the flags of the states surrounding Israel are the same colours of the flags the four horsemen of the Apocalypse. The bottom line as Jesus says, is that nobody really knows, so we must be constantly ready.

Another way is thinking of this is that Jesus has already come and is still with us as the Holy Spirit. This would square with His words that some of the current generation would see Him (Matthew 24.34). The key point is we will all see Him and face judgement either at the end time or when we die.

Liberalism doesn't like to hear about divine judgement and harsh punishment. This is a natural human reaction to the sad history of church leaders trying to scare people into the Kingdom. Human rights tribunals in Canada have found a pastor guilty of hate speech for teaching "Anyone whose name was not written in the book of life was thrown into the lake of fire" (Revelation 20:14). Personally, I would appreciate the warning, time to "come to Jesus" and avoid this fate. I would argue that not warning people is more hateful, or at least a failure to love.

Extreme liberal Christians tend to assume, contrary to Jesus' teaching, that God's love and mercy always trump sin guilt. This assumption overturns everything the Bible teaches about God's holiness, righteousness (right relationship) and justice.

Belief in a serious final judgement is our motivation to love God and our neighbour, keep God's Commandments and avoid sin. This is why believers act differently than non-believers. Believers can generally be trusted with freedom, sustain democratic government and be successful in business. This is why cultures built on these beliefs are the most socially, politically, and economically progressive cultures of the world. The reason we are in social, political, and economic chaos is because liberalism has deceived many people into a false Christianity.

3.6: "I believe in the Holy Spirit,"

The challenge is not just believing in the Holy Spirit but believing in what the Bible says about the Holy Spirit. As a cradle Anglican, I cannot remember ever hearing a teaching on the Holy Spirit. I came to believe in the Holy Spirit during the Charismatic revival that swept Western Canada in the late 70s. My faith went from confusion to real belief through my experiences of hearing singing in tongues, being slain in the Spirit, spiritual healing, and a real baptism in the Holy Spirit. I had read the whole Bible more than once and was angry that nobody had ever told me about the Holy Spirit in Church. I graduated with a rather pompous Master of Divinity degree and was ordained with almost no teaching on the Holy Spirit. I have been learning and teaching about the Holy Spirit for the last 30 years as a priest at www.spirituallifeteaching.info.

Jesus promised the disciples He would send the Holy Spirit to help them after His death, Resurrection and Ascension. The Holy Spirit is the continuing presence of Jesus on earth. The word "holy" should be a clue. The Holy Spirit will come and live in our personal Spirit, as Jesus in us. The dative case in Greek means physically inside. But first we must create a holy, sin-free space in our personal spirit. We also must invite the Holy Spirit. Remember, God has given us free will.

The Holy Spirit is our guide, teacher, conscience, comforter, and healer. When our spiritual eyes are opened by the Holy Spirit of Jesus, we see the pain, suffering, evil, deception and woundedness all around us.

Extreme liberalism generally dismisses the whole supernatural worldview of the Bible as superstition, mythical or exaggerated legend. Healing and deliverance ministry has been lost in most churches. I am challenging clergy and pastors who lack experience in healing and deliverance ministry to up their game by reading John and Paula Sandford's book *Healing and Deliverance* or my *Going Spiritual*, attending a workshop and getting involved in this core Christian ministry. The Holy Spirit is at the heart of the supernatural dimension of the Bible that extreme liberalism has dismissed as mythical. The Holy Spirit as the presence of Jesus is one of the seven lost spiritual truths of the Foundation churches must teach if we are to recover truth freedom, and democracy.

3.7: "…the holy catholic Church, the communion of saints,"

The holy catholic (small c) church includes all the believers who are in the New Covenant of Jesus as defined by the Apostles' Creed. The Roman Catholic Church claims exclusive authority because the Bible says Jesus appointed Peter the leader of His Church (Matthew. 16:19). While this is literally true, and the Pope is generally respected as the senior leader of the Christian Church, other churches are in various degrees of accepting his authority. The reason is the Roman Catholic Church, and specifically its historical leadership; became politicized, intellectualized, corrupted, and at least temporarily lost their spiritual authority.

The Roman Catholic Church grew and spread out all over the known world with equal patriarchs in Rome, Constantinople, Alexandria, Antioch, and Jerusalem. The Orthodox Church of Constantinople split off from Rome and then became divided into Patriarchs and national churches in Greece, Turkey, Ukraine, and Russia. The Protestant Reformation further divided the Church into national churches, and then further divisions, as different Protestant churches split off. The holy catholic church is now a spiritual (not political) communion of believers who are under the authority of Jesus and led by the Holy Spirit of Jesus.

Holiness is an ancient word that is rarely talked about or understood by modern Christians. The Biblical story of Moses at Mt. Sinai includes a divine warning that the (unholy) people must not even touch the base of the mountain or "He will break out against them" (Exodus 19.24). The point is that God's love and holiness is like a divine fire that would consume anything unholy that came into His holy presence. A practical example would be to think of our soul as a container, and our sins as drops of gasoline in the container. If our soul came into the holy fire of God's presence, it would be like an open can of gasoline being brought too close to a raging campfire — not pretty.

The Church is to be holy. Holy means whole, undivided, other, unpolluted, and pure. St. John gives us a definition of heaven as excluding "...the cowardly, the unbelieving, the vile, murderers, the sexually immoral, those who practice magic arts, the idolaters and all liars..." (Revelation 21:8). Their destiny is a second spiritual death and anguish of being eternally excluded from being in God's presence.

Many churches have been liberalized, politicalized, divided, intellectualized, and fail to meet these ideals. This is why they are divided, considered irrelevant by seekers and serious believers and declining.

Extreme liberalism does not accept the authority of biblical teachings on holiness and sexual immorality. This has placed Christian pastors and priests and church leaders in a very difficult position for the last 30 years. They want to love and affirm all men and women as equally beloved children (by adoption) of God and proclaim (not just affirm) the good news of forgiveness in Jesus. The challenge is that forgiveness is dependent on repentance and belief in Jesus — i.e., what the Bible says. Extreme liberalism sees no need to repent what the Bible describes as unholy sexual immorality because it does not accept the spiritual truths of the Bible.

Sexual immorality is why extreme liberal LGBTQ woke activists had to deconstruct the biblical foundation of spiritual truths in the Bible that limited their personal freedom on sexual morality. This is the selfish coward's way out. It is deconstructing the faith of the many so the few can do whatever they like. They have liberated the minority and imprisoned the majority in a false, powerless Christianity. Extreme liberalism has upended what the church teaches, so those who do not want to live holy lives, do not have to face the fact that they have chosen to put themselves out of a right-relationship with God and possibly eternal spiritual life.

The communion of saints is all the believers on earth or in heaven who are included in the Covenant of Jesus. The Holy Communion service in traditional churches is a celebration of our redemption and inclusion. It intentionally includes Bible teaching, the Creed, and a time for confession of sins and absolution from an ordained priest or minister. This is preparation for participation in receiving the consecrated bread and wine to nourish and strengthen our spiritual life. Holy Communion is a visible gathering of the saints on earth celebrating their union with Jesus and the saints in heaven. It is also an opportunity for those who have fallen away to come home and re-connect with the Covenant community.

3.8: "…the forgiveness of sins,"

The forgiveness of sins is the Good News of the Covenant of Jesus mentioned above. Sin is any failure to love God and our neighbour. The Ten Commandments (Exodus 20:1–17) summarize how we can test our love. We do not love God exclusively if we love other gods (i.e. money, power, hockey, sex), if we use God's name frivolously, worship idols, fail to set aside a sabbath day to honour God, or if we dishonour our parents (God's teachers). We obviously fail to love our neighbour if we murder, commit adultery, steal, lie (false witness), or covet (wrongfully want) anything that belongs to our neighbour.

The Church has traditionally taught the Seven Deadly Sins as: pride, greed, lust, envy, gluttony, wrath, and sloth. This includes the invisible failures to love, like murder in the heart (hate and gossip). Sin pollutes our personal spirit, makes us unholy and can exclude us from the Covenant of Jesus. Jesus gave the Church the authority to forgive sins.

> *"Therefore, confess your sins to each other and pray for each other so that you may be healed,"*
>
> *James 5:16*

The Anglican, Roman Catholic and Orthodox churches have traditionally claimed this authority exclusively for ordained priests under the seal of The Confession. It has been the most powerful and joyful part of my healing ministry for 30 years.

The essence and fatal flaw of extreme liberalism is that it does not believe in the supernatural dimension of the Bible. This includes Satan, spiritual evil, and the seriousness of sin. This works for Satan but not so well for the rest of us.

Many liberals in the Church reject sin and judgement as limiting human freedom. It does. But a healthy fear of judgement is what creates the trust, co-operation and order all free countries and progressive democracies depend on.

Liberalism sees God as love. Contrary to the central message of the Bible, extreme liberals think of God's love and mercy as somehow overriding the need for personal repentance and confession and forgiveness. This is an example of how our human mind can deceive us. Liberals tend to see God more as "in the forgiveness business" than being holy. They assume (that word again) God just forgives people. This is a self-serving error of logic.

At the other end of the religious spectrum, many evangelicals tend to think (very non-biblically), that all they must do is make a single decision and accept Jesus as their Saviour to achieve automatic lifelong immunity from sins. They stare at me blankly if I suggest this is a non-biblical denominational teaching. They are just as vulnerable to temptation and sin as extreme liberals. I know this because I have seen demons being spiritually cast out of good, "Bible believing" Christian evangelicals.

The differences between Liberalism, and what the Bible teaches about the holiness of God and the sacrificial death of Jesus as full payment of the sins of the world, shows liberalism to be a false Christianity.

3.9: "…the resurrection of the body, and …life everlasting."

The Resurrection of Jesus (explained above) gives believing Christians the hope that there is an eternal spiritual life after death. The biblical accounts teach us that the Risen Jesus had a body that seemed to be both material and immaterial. Jesus could pass through locked doors (John 20:19, 27), eat food (Acts 1:3) and be touched (John 20:27). Our resurrection body is changed, made incorruptible and raised spiritually. (1 Corinthians 15:42–44).

To understand our own resurrection and life everlasting, we need to understand the body-soul-spirit relationship. These words are used to mean different things by different authors. The most helpful author is Watchman Nee, whose teachings have been assembled and published by his students in *The Spiritual Man.*

My insight came from the second creation story in Genesis, where God forms the man out of clay and then breaths the breath of life into the man (Genesis 2:7). This is illustrated on the cover of, *Going Spiritual,* by a blue circle, God's breath or Spirit overlapping a red circle (body). The purple overlap in the middle represents the soul.

Our personal spirit is our intuitive mind which senses truth, lies, guilt, love, joy, and peace. This is where the Holy Spirit, the Spirit of Jesus and of transcendent truth can come and live in us if we invite Him. We experience this as our conscience. Women are generally more intuitive than men and "just know" if you really love them. Men struggle to figure it out in their rational minds — in the soul.

The soul is the meat in the sandwich. This is where the sensing desires of our spirit compete for sovereignty with the physical and ego desires of our body. Our will is in our soul and serves as the arbitrator between giving priority to our bodily ego desires, or to our spiritual desires. When we ignore the desire of our spirit to be in right-relationship with God and our neighbour; we sin and pollute our spirit. The pollution of sin weakens our spirit. A life of sin can lead to spiritual bondage and even spiritual death. Our polluted spirit may not be able to carry our soul to heaven when we die physically. It remains buried in the ground with our body. There may be no resurrection and no eternal spiritual life. This is why being a Christian believer and included in the Covenant of Jesus with the possibility of forgiveness of sins, is so important.

Extreme liberalism is very squishy on what happens when we die. This is awkward for more orthodox clergy and pastors at funerals, where everyone is in grief because poor old sinner, George has died. Telling the truth — that George is just dead and missed out on an eternal life of joy because he was not a believer — is seen as very unkind. We tend to become more liberal ourselves and talk vaguely about George being such a good and kind person, that a God of love would surely welcome him into heaven. Fudging the truth gets us through a difficult time at funerals, but any misleading teaching will be very hard to explain to Jesus when we die.

One of the best teachings on what happens at death is the interviews with Howard Storm, *Howard Storm Died, Went to Hell, and Came Back,* on YouTube at:

```
youtu.be/b9f2n0xPZ3k?si=7ZFY0tvBePsj7p-W
```

Howard Storm was an American atheist art professor married to an atheist. While in Paris, he had severe food poisoning. He experienced death, his soul leaving his body, and being carried off by demons to hell and tortured. While in constant excruciating pain and being savagely bitten by the demons, he remembered fragments of the Lord's Prayer and the Psalm 23 that his grandmother had taught him. While deliriously mumbling these, he saw a light coming toward him. Jesus carried him up to heaven and talked to him for a half hour before his body was resuscitated by doctors. His atheist wife left him, and he became a Christian pastor in California.

Many people in our time have had visions of heaven and shared them on YouTube and in books. This is the Good News of the resurrection of the body and life everlasting.

3.10: Recovering the Foundation of Truth

We urgently need to recover the Judeo-Christian foundation of spiritual truth — the absolute truths on which western freedom, democracy, and economic prosperity are based. I explain them in the context of Chapter 9 (page 145) This does not mean everyone has to become a believer. We must respect God's gift of personal freedom to love and obey God — or not. It does mean that there needs to be a majority or consensus in the culture who know and respect these truths as having divine authority and serious personal consequences.

Compare the thriving democracies in U.K., U.S., Canada, Australia, France, Germany, and Israel, with the totalitarianism of China, Pakistan, Afghanistan, Myanmar, Iran, and Saudi Arabia. The painful legacy of long, costly, and destructive wars in Vietnam and Afghanistan should have taught us that you cannot help or force people that do not have this cultural foundation of Judeo-Christian spiritual truth to develop into a socially progressive, free, and democratic country.

Recovering this foundation of spiritual truths in our Western culture will not be easy. I have summarized how this can be done in Chapter 9 by:

1. Challenging church leaders to teach and affirm the seven lost spiritual truths of the Foundation.

2. Challenging public schools, universities and colleges to affirm the Judeo-Christian spiritual truths and teach objective truth.

Challenging churches to teach the foundation of supernatural truths of the foundation is the first, most important and most difficult task. This is a call for deeper theological thinking in many churches. Church leaders need to be challenged by members to consider the seven lost spiritual truths, identify which ones they are not teaching, overcome their denominationalism and intellectualism, and begin teaching these lost spiritual truths.

As motivation I humbly point out that God's order of creation works on survival of the fittest. Jordan Peterson's Rule #4 in *Beyond Order* is: "Observe that opportunity lurks where responsibility has been abandoned." Peterson regularly attracts about 2,000 people in a large city to hear a message that is highly relevant to modern life and biblical. Church leaders with dwindling congregations need to reflect on this.

The Good News is that God always preserves a remnant — a few faithful believers. Others are observing the order and joy in their lives, joining them, and that church is growing. This is happening in our time as many new leaders are raised up, and many new, thriving churches are emerging. Traditional churches that are teaching these seven lost spiritual truths are also growing rapidly. The success of Jordan Peterson's book, *12 Rules for Life* (5 million copies), should wake church leaders up to the spiritual destruction of woke liberalism, the huge demand for orthodox spiritual teaching, and the way forward for modern churches and serious Christians.

4: Climate Emergency as False Science

Figures don't lie, but liars do figure.

anonymous

Climate Emergency as False Science is the second example of a woke false truth determined by flawed human reason that is driving our post-truth culture into social and economic chaos. We will examine the science and expose the sad political history of fake climate emergencies from Al Gore's infamous mathematical error leading to a dramatic increase in global warming, to Germany and California's disastrous experiments with wind and solar. Climate Emergency is the most tangible example of objective scientific data being manipulated, politicized and weaponized for political and corporate gain.

When politicians say the science is settled, they are lying. *Unsettled* is the title of one of the books we will be examining. The science is only settled in the minds of a minority of politicalized scientists, activists, and opportunistic politicians. Politicians know the silent majority is sleeping and only starts to pay attention to issues at election time. This is the fatal flaw in Western democracy. Democracy depends on voters staying informed and voting wisely. Politicians have learned that if a lie is repeated often enough, people will believe it.

Climate emergency is a false truth that has been used for a power grab by the woke New Left Marxist environmentalist elite. We will expose the political danger and the social and economic cost of the anti-capitalist policies that are being justified by this false science. The title and sub-title of Bjorn Lombard's book, *False Alarm: How climate change panic costs us trillions, hurts the poor, and fails to fix the planet* says it all.[27]

We will begin by examining the causes of global warming — the real science. Hint: it's not CO_2 emissions. We will learn global warming and cooling happens in cycles over long time periods, and that it is caused by a natural balance of factors, including distance from the sun, cloud and smoke cover, greenhouse gases, and ground cover reflection.

How is global warming measured? This is also complex and includes five different types of measurement — ground stations, ocean buoys, low and high-altitude balloons, and satellite imaging. The challenge is how to average this all out as these measurements are not evenly distributed and are affected by proximity to natural heat domes in urban areas.

Global warming and cooling occur naturally in long cycles that have been measured for thousands of years. Where I sit in Calgary has been under a mile of glacial ice (cold period) and is two hours from Drumheller where dinosaur bones have been discovered (hot period).

Once we understand the basic science, we will move on to examine how these measurements have been projected forward from 1975 by multiple flawed computer models overseen by the Intergovernmental Panel on Climate Change (IPCC). All these computer models are programmed using assumptions (that word again) about the relative influence of the multiple factors influencing both warming and cooling. By comparing the computer-generated projections from 1975 to 2020, to the measured global temperatures, we will see that the model projections are consistently much higher than the actual temperature increase — and that the models are not "fit for purpose."

We will also expose the false science of:

1. Melting glaciers and rising oceans

2. Extreme weather, fires, and floods

3. Wind and solar power and

4. Magical electric cars.

The solemn-faced newscasters who assure us every time there is a hurricane, flood, or forest fire — because of global warming — are wrong. They are repeating a script written by the New Left Marxist environmentalists for their anti-capitalist and anti-oil agenda. The science is only settled in the minds of those who use it to gain political power. It's Al Gore all over again. The only difference is the New Left Marxist environmentalist elite has a different, hidden, expensive and scary agenda. In Section *4.8: Climate Disaster in Germany and the U.S.*, we will examine in detail how this elite came to political power in Germany in 1998, wasted 304 billion euros on solar power subsidies, bankrupted the three largest power utilities and raised the cost of power to 3.5 times the cost in America. CO_2 emissions from German power companies rose by 5%.

4.1: What Causes Global Warming?

"The science shows us that fears of climate apocalypse are unfounded. Global warming is real, but it is not the end of the world. It is a manageable problem. Yet we live in a world where almost half the population believes climate change will extinguish humanity".[28]

The false science of the IPCC computer models assumes (that word again) major increases in CO_2 emissions. This is because the New Left Marxists and environmentalists influencing the scientists generating the models are anti-oil. We need to examine the real science to understand how the earth is warmed and how it is cooled. There is a delicate natural balance between the many variables that affect heating and cooling greenhouse gases. This includes CO_2, which "accounts for about 7% of the atmosphere's ability to intercept heat."[29]

The heat from the sun is not a constant. It varies according to orbital distance from the sun and solar flare activity. This variation has not been researched thoroughly enough. It is not in the computer models and could be a significant cause and variable. Global warming is out of our hands to "fight." It is a known unknown.

About 30% of solar heat is reflected into space before reaching earth.[30] Water vapour (clouds) accounts for more than 90% of the atmosphere's ability to intercept heat.[31] One Swedish study has seriously investigated the costs/benefits of a massive fleet of boats spraying sea water into the atmosphere to prevent the social and economic damage done by global warming. More heat is reflected from light-coloured roofs, buildings, and roads. Researchers have investigated the idea of painting asphalt roofs and pavement in light colours. Developed farmland and pasture reflects more heat than forests. We are beginning to see the complexity of all these variables. Forests both absorb more heat and lead to cooling by absorbing the CO_2 and other greenhouse gases that slow heat loss to space. CO_2 is heavier than air. It mostly falls to the ground and is an essential plant food.

Aerosols (fine particles) in the air also reflect heat. Burning low quality coal, forest fires and volcanos, for example, can have a measurable effect on reducing the amount of heat reaching the surface. Stephen Koonin gives the example of Mt. Pinatubo erupting in 1991, which cooled the earth by 0.6° C for 15 months.[32]

The earth is cooled as this heat from the sun is radiated into the atmosphere and then into space. This is where greenhouse gases come into the picture. Heat travels in the form of radio-like waves. Different lengths of waves can be blocked by the molecules in specific greenhouse gases. The reason for all the focus on carbon dioxide is that this tiny molecule can block waves of a specific length, and about 7% of the heat vented into space.

The concentration of CO_2 in the atmosphere has increased from 280 ppm (parts per million) in 1750 to 410 ppm in 2019. Koonin estimates this increase in CO_2 has increased the amount of heat intercepted in the atmosphere from 82.1% in 1750 to 82.7% in 2019 — a 0.6% increase! The point is that yes, CO_2 emissions and humans burning fossil fuels are drivers, but not the main driver of global warming. The important question is to find a way forward that balances the need to slow this warming without limiting political freedom and the economic growth needed to fund remediation measures, social programs, and food aid for millions of people. If there was a sudden new increase in global temperature, additional trillions of dollars would be needed for remediating this damage.

4.2: How Do We Measure Global Warming?

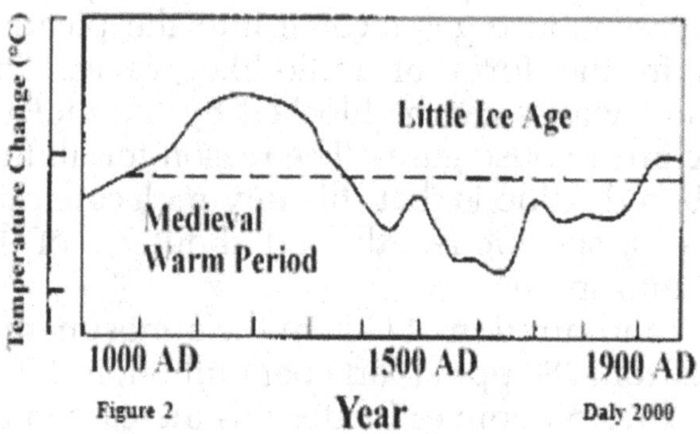

Figure 1: Source: "First IPCC Report, 1990," in Climate Change Science Essay *by Ken Gregory,* friendsofscience.org, *downloaded Sept 25, 2023.*

Global warming happens in geological time, measured in thousands of years. Measuring global warming is extremely complicated. For example, how do you measure the temperature of the ocean, which covers two-thirds of the planet? Measurement is complicated by the fact that most of the recording stations are in the more developed, northern hemisphere countries, at airports. These airports are near growing major cities that have temperatures around them normally two° C above the surrounding rural areas.

Climate includes the 10,000 feet above the earth, which has been measured by weather balloons for decades. More technically advanced countries have developed satellite imaging techniques to measure surface temperatures from space, and radio-equipped buoys to drop in oceans to measure temperatures. The ideal scenario would be to get agreement on how to average out all these measurements to get a reliable global average, which is really a "best guess." Instead, scientists report variations from the historical measurements from a base year. The selection of a base year (1979), when temperatures were naturally rising from a low, is what has led to a scientifically false climate emergency. This was intentional and unprofessional, as the IPCC scientists would have known this was in a period of natural global warming. They would have known that warming began in 1850, long before CO_2 producing cars were invented. The real science disproves the false New Left Marxist environmentalist science of a human-caused climate emergency caused by increased CO_2. This is New Left Marxism by stealth, not science.

4.3: How Computer Models Project Higher Temperatures

The computerized climate models used to develop estimates of future global warming are extremely complex. They include hard to measure variables such as aerosols in the atmosphere that reflect solar heat back into space and reduce warming. Changes in land use from forests to pastures also reflect more heat and reduces warming. These models make dozens of assumptions about how human activity, demographic changes, industrialization, and economic development will affect global warming. The result is that "…the later generation of models is more uncertain than the earlier ones. The fact that the spread in their results is increasing is as good evidence as any that the science is far from settled."[33]

Christie's graph in Figure 2 , below, compares the average of 102 IPCC model projections with the observed measurements from balloons and satellite measurements since 1979.[34] The IPCC model projections differ from the observed temperatures by their flawed assumption of greenhouse gasses and, particularly CO_2, causing warming.

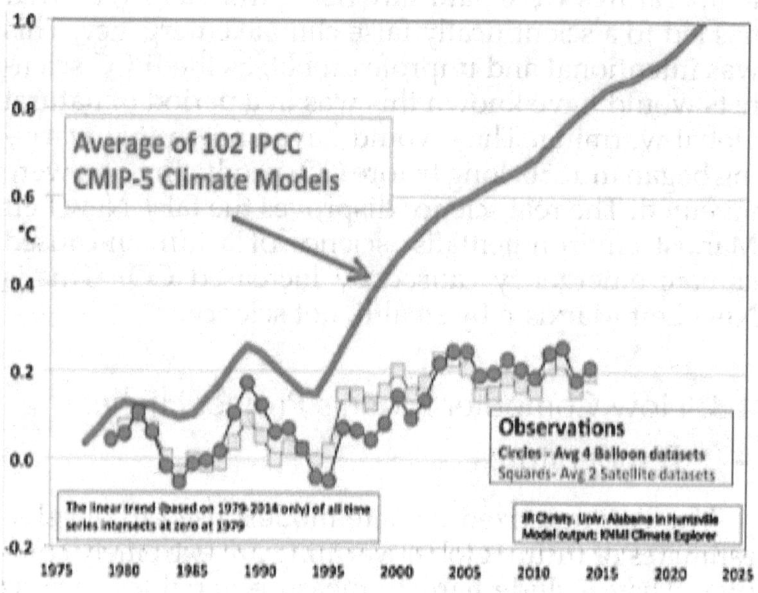

Figure 2: Tropical Mid-Tropospheric Temperature Variations Models vs. Observation. Source: John R. Christie, 29 March 2017 testimony to U.S. House Committee on Science, Space & Technology.

A rise in global temperature of 1.1° C in 120 years is about half of that projected by the various computer models used by the UN Intergovernmental Panel on Climate Change. Their Special Report on Emission Scenarios in the year 2000 studied six scenarios, with assumptions ranging from "doing nothing" to reducing net carbon emissions to net zero by the year 2050. The IPCC's projected "doing nothing" assumption would lead to a computer projected increase in global warming of about 4.0° C by 2050. The IPCC's net zero CO_2 emissions by 2050 assumption, which creates the most economically disruptive scenario, would lead to a global warming increase of about 1.8° C. This net zero by 2050 IPCC scenario has become the internationally agreed political goal on which the Paris Climate Accord climate "emergency" hangs.

Since the IPCC computer models assume (wrongly) that human CO_2 emissions are the major cause; there is only one way this "emergency" could be solved. That would be to institute a massive \$270.00/ton, internationally imposed and verifiable carbon tax, a rapid conversion to magical electric cars and (ineffective) wind and solar power and the deconstruction of the oil and gas industry. As we will see in the following sections, this outcome will be proven to be scientifically unfeasible and economically ruinous. Germany wasted trillions of dollars on this strategy, and CO_2 emissions increased.

These theoretical scenarios and computer projections are dramatically higher than the temperatures measured in the last century, when CO_2 emissions increased by 30%.[35] In the words of Swedish climate scientist Fritz Vahrenholt:

> *"There is no doubt that the community of states will have to react in the course of this century and reduce CO_2 emissions. However, the faulty climate models must not be used for this. They run 50% too hot compared to that in reality. That means we have twice as much time. Not in 2050, but in 2100, do we have to say goodbye to fossil fuels to a large extent."[36]*

The problem is that the science has been politicized and distorted by focusing on the human causes of global warming, excluding the natural causes. The UN Framework Convention on Climate Change specifically defines climate change as

"...a change in climate which is attributed directly or indirectly to human activity that alters the composition of the global atmosphere, and which is in addition to natural climate variability observed over comparable time periods...."[37]

"The real question is not whether the globe has warmed recently, but rather, to what extent is this warming being caused by humans."[38] The point is we cannot have a useful conversation about "the science" without examining the measured temperatures in geological time — thousands of years. The models are only as good as the assumptions on which they are built. Because the politicized IPCC's assumed CO_2 emissions measurements have been proven to be incorrect, this invalidates the resulting projections of a climate emergency. Koonin (above) calculated that CO_2 accounts for about 7% of the atmosphere's ability to intercept heat and has caused 0.6% of the increase in global warming. In 2019 an international group of over 500 climate scientists (USA, Sweden, Irish Republic, Italy, France, Germany, and the UK) wrote to the Secretary General of the UN and Secretary of the United Nations Framework Convention on Climate Change. They requested a formal discussion of the IPCC climate models. They stated:

"The general circulation models of climate on which international policy is at present founded are unfit for their purpose. Therefore, it is cruel and unwise to advocate the spending of trillions of dollars on the basis of results from such immature models. Current climate policies pointlessly and grievously undermine the economic system, putting lives at risk in

In their request they asked to meet with the IPCC scientists to sort this out. Their appeal has been ignored.

4.4: Melting Glaciers and Rising Oceans

Al Gore's 2006 film *An Inconvenient Truth* set the stage for the false science of global warming. His graphic images of baby polar bears at sea on melting ice floes, melting glaciers, and New York under thirty-two feet of water, got everyone's attention and made him a millionaire. Despite serious criticism of the mathematics in the models he cited, he is still jetting to climate conferences all over the world, spewing out tons of CO_2 on the way. It was a couple of Canadians who checked the math and found a basic mathematical error that would get anyone a failing grade in university. Figures don't lie, but liars do figure. The threat of melting glaciers and rising oceans is still the first go-to argument of the climate extremists. What does the real science say? Swedish climate scientist and former IPCC member, Bjorn Lomborg, gives us the short answer: "In fact, sea levels have risen about a foot in the past 150 years."[40] What the climate alarmists ignore is that sea levels, and natural global warming, have been rising and falling for millions of years.

Koonin puts sea level variations in the context of the last 400,000 years:

> *"Four point-two million years ago, these sea levels were 140 meters below present levels. They were about twenty meters above present levels about 140,000 years ago".*[41]

The most obvious, and hilarious, way to prove the false science of global warming and sea level change is to put an ice cube in a full glass of water and wait for it to melt. As Lawson says, "The melting of floating polar ice clearly cannot cause any rise in sea levels — just as the melting of ice cubes in your glass of water cannot cause the water to overflow the glass."[42]

There is some truth in the rising-sea argument. If there is significantly more glacier melting on land than accumulating, this water could raise sea levels slightly. This needs to be kept in perspective, as two-thirds of the earth is ocean, so there is lots of room where the water can spread out. Al Gore showed dramatic evidence that glaciers were melting worldwide. This melting has continued but is offset by cooler temperatures in other parts of the world. For example, Lawson notes that:

> "...the West Antarctica ice sheet...is showing signs of melting and glacier retreat...in most of the other 90% of the continent ...the ice sheet appears to be growing."[43]

> "...while there has been some slight warming in this century [in Greenland]...temperatures are still below levels of the1930s and 1940s."[44]

Coastal flooding is hyped as the main challenge of global warming, and the one that could require trillions of dollars in remediation funding, if true. But it isn't true. Continents have risen and fallen for millions of years. People have learned to adapt. Sadly, the hype of this false science goes on. Lomborg shares the humorous story of the UN Secretary General being photographed in his suit and tie off the low-lying Polynesian island of Tuvalu, with water up to his waist to dramatize ocean rise. The real science for the island, as reported in *Nature Magazine,* "...confirms sea level rising but total land area expanding by 2.4%."[45] Lomborg explains that wave action washing sand up on beaches leads to this accretion and growth in land area.

4.5: Extreme Weather, Fires and Flooding

This false science is deeply embedded in our post-truth culture. Every news report of extreme weather, fire and flooding disaster ends with the supposedly informed scientific observation that this is yet another example of the coming carnage of global warming. In contrast, statements from the IPCC's AR5 WGI Report, indicating what we don't know, include:

- Trends in the magnitude or frequency of floods on a global scale

- Trends in drought, hail, thunderstorms.

- Large scale changes in the intensity of extreme tropical cyclones since 1900.[46]

Koonin shares a very telling story from his time as a scientist with the US Government. President Obama was deeply into the false science of global warming and requested a Climate Assessment in 2017. The Report, of course, came back with high confidence that:

> *"There have been marked changes in temperature extremes across the contiguous United States. The number of temperature records set in the past two decades far exceed the number of low temperature records."*[47]

Koonin contacted a colleague who checked the data using the absolute high and low temperatures of 725 US weather stations and calculated the actual variations from 1931. The opposite was found to be true:

> *"Christie's analysis of absolute warms and colds showed…that temperature extremes in the contiguous US have become less common and somewhat milder since the late Nineteenth Century."*[48]

Christie's analysis implies that the official Report had used a flawed mathematical model (as did Al Gore) to calculate results that would automatically show an increase. Governments hire political staff for a reason.

Hurricanes are the most dramatic example of extreme weather and cause enormous damage. Solemn-faced newscasters automatically attribute the massive damage to global warming. What we don't consider is that the coastal population of Florida for example, has increased by 67 times; so of course, there is much more damage. Lomborg gives us the short answer:

> *"The UN's climate scientists looked at the evidence and concluded that globally hurricanes are not getting more frequent."*[49]

There was a horrific forest fire in Fort McMurray, Alberta in 2016, which destroyed about half the town, and was automatically blamed on global warming. Some, who probably don't even believe in God, saw it as God's judgement on the town as the hub of the "evil" Alberta oilsands. We get tired of celebrities jetting over Fort McMurray in private jets spewing out tons of CO_2 emissions and condemning the cleanest and most carbon-efficient oil industry in the world.

Anyone with access to Google Maps and Street View could see the real cause of the huge natural forest fire overwhelming Fort McMurray. There were wooden houses with wooden outbuildings within a stone's (or spark's) throw of an unusually dry and unmanaged forest. The town was surrounded by hundreds of miles of very dry pine forests, with no (provincial) fire breaks, and no city bylaws on how close you could build to the forest. The main causes of increased forest fire damage are poor forest management, urban sprawl, and wooden buildings with flammable roofs too close to the forest edge.[50] According to Lomborg, the bottom line on wildfires is:

> *"In total, the global amount of area burned has declined more than 540,000 sq. mi., from 1.9 million sq. mi. in the early part of the last century to 1.4 million sq. mi.[51]*

Lomborg believes we should take protective measures against wildfires seriously as global warming, if it continues, could increase the risk of forest fires through this century. But he notes that, as with flooding, "…the best way to manage fires is to focus not on carbon dioxide levels but on human behavior."[52] The reason the damage is increasing is because populations and buildings are multiplying. The lack of proper fire breaks around houses and outbuildings, and poor construction with flammable roofing and siding materials is the real cause.

4.6: Wind and Solar

The problem with depending on wind and solar power is the science. Electricity cannot be stored economically or efficiently. It must be produced on demand and at the same time as it is consumed. Storing electricity in batteries "...is not a little more expensive but tens of thousands of times more expensive than storing gas in tanks or coal beside power plants."[60] Wind, and solar power are not reliable and must always be supported by fossil-fuelled backup generators. These in turn increase net CO_2 emissions, cancelling out the lower emissions of wind and solar.

Another problem with the science of wind power is that it is often produced in remote areas requiring the construction of new long-distance transmission lines to connect to the electrical grid. Lomborg notes:

> *"The interconnectedness of the grid means that everything depends on and affects everything else on it."*[53]

The constant turning on and off, of backup generators increases the cost of maintenance, reduces their efficiency and makes dependence on large scale wind and solar power prohibitively expensive.

Wind and solar power are not as environmentally green as you might think. There are significant CO_2 emissions from the fossil-fuel driven machinery used in mining and shipping the rare minerals that batteries are made of. Fossil fuel is also used in manufacturing the solar panels, turbine blades and storage batteries. The panels and blades have a 20-year lifespan. They are not recyclable and are already a waste management problem.

A huge number of birds are killed each year by wind turbine blades, or by having their wings singed by flying over huge solar farms. One 2013 study cited in *Forbes* estimated that there were 573,000 bird kills each year from wind farms.[54]

The bottom line is that wind and solar power is still only one of the many developing technologies, including small nuclear, hydrogen, fission, and fusion. These technologies all may have a viable place in global emission reduction in the future, if needed. At present we would have to depend on proven technologies like nuclear, hydro, geothermal, natural gas, and carbon capture for immediate emission reduction.

To put the false science of wind and solar in perspective, Rupert Darwell states that despite over:

> *"...140 billion every year in government subsidies for inefficient wind and solar power...these renewable sources produced only about one percent of global energy needs."*[55]

In the longer term, the International Energy Agency estimates that "...by 2040 and even after another \$4 trillion has been spent on subsidies, solar and wind power will deliver only 5% of global energy needs."[56]

The *National Post* (February 4, 2022) published a report disclosing discrepancies in the production numbers of megawatts of electricity in Alberta. On a windy day on the prairies Alberta's largest wind farm in Black Spring Ridge, rated as producing 300 MW was producing "...only 56 MW, according to Alberta Electric System Operator data." It would be a tragic pun to say solar, and wind are "overrated."

4.7: Magical Electric Cars

Popular thinking about electric cars is best described as "magical thinking" by Lomborg. The only science involved, as far as most people are concerned, is zero CO_2 emissions. They ignore the lifecycle emissions of mining, transporting, and manufacturing the car. They ignore emissions from electricity production, is efficiently stored in batteries, and assume it is available anywhere. An average gasoline car emits thirty-four tons of CO_2 over its lifetime (including CO_2 emitted for its manufacture). An electric car emits twenty-six tons of CO_2 over its lifetime. The real lifecycle science says that switching from an average gasoline car to an electric car only reduces total CO_2 emissions by 24%.[57]

Sadly, electricity does not grow on trees. It must be generated and come from somewhere (probably with CO_2 emissions) and get to where it is needed and used in the same moment. As mentioned above, storing energy in batteries is tens of thousands of times less efficient than storing gasoline. Exponentially more power generation and related CO_2 emissions are involved. Then, there is the problem of recycling. I almost bought a hybrid. But when I found out the huge weight of batteries had to be replaced after about 10 years at a cost of thousands of dollars, I changed my mind. Producing batteries includes mining dangerous rare minerals (lithium), shipping them overseas to a polluting chemical plant, then shipping them to a car manufacturer — often in different countries. This is where the extra CO_2 emissions come from. Lithium is described by a climate scientist friend as "the most dangerous substance on the planet and explodes at -40° F." Not the sort of thing we would like to have parked outside our house on a very cold winter day in Alberta. These are some of the things the woke environmentalist activists didn't tell you.

The final challenge with the science of electric cars is public recharging stations. A statement from Toyota warns that the grid and infrastructure simply aren't there to support the electrification of the private car fleet. A 2017 U.S. Government study found that about

8,500 strategically placed charge stations would be needed to support a fleet of just 7 million electric vehicles.[58] This would be about six times the current number of electric cars. It is way below the 300 million needed over the next twenty years if GM and other carmakers follow through on promises to eliminate internal combustion engines.

These recharging stations must be more robust than what you have at home. Home charging takes three to eight hours. Lomborg points out that the best-case-scenario fast charging (30 minutes) cannot be done on home power. It uses direct current and specialized systems". Even 30 minutes would create intolerable frustration and huge lineups for people used to spending five minutes filling their cars with gas. Lomborg notes:

"The International Energy Agency hopes we can reach 130 million electric cars by 2030 (from 5 million in 2020) ...it would cut a trifling 0.4 percent of global emissions by 2030."[59]

The folly continues as the U.S. and Canada have both decided to become green superpowers by investing hundreds of billion dollars in battery factories and green infrastructure. Recent experience has shown that consumers are rejecting electrical vehicles as too expensive. Cheaper Chinese imports are taxed at 100% to protect North American sales and piling up in storage. This is clearly, like wind and solar power, the unnecessary and wrong way to go about slowing down global warming.

4.8: Climate Disaster in Germany and the U.S.

Nietzsche and Dostoyevsky warned that the loss of belief in a divine authority for truth would lead to social chaos and the rise of totalitarianism. The warning came true in Germany. Rupert Darwall says that a dark coalition of radical New Left Marxists, environmentalists, socialists, and former Nazis gained and used their political power to implement disastrous anti-capitalist economic policies. These policies were not effective in reducing CO_2 emissions. This was the first step in their hidden agenda of replacing free market capitalism and democracy with government by a "progressive" totalitarian elite — themselves. The silent majority needs to know how this happened and replace the irresponsible politicians. This is a key step in recovering a thriving economic foundation of truth, freedom, and democracy.

German politicians and green activists saw the success of Al Gore in getting attention by presenting scary photos of melting glaciers, rising oceans and the fraudulent hockey stick graph showing temperatures rising so fast he had to go up on a lift to point at the future. They also remembered the clever "acid rain" panic of Olaf Palm, who swept to political power in Sweden by working with environmentalists. The German Socialists, Greens, New Left Marxists, and other extremists all had an anti-industrial and pro-environmental bond. Senior civil servants, scientists and journalists all saw an opportunity to get ahead. The emerging wind and solar industries were not economically viable without huge subsidies. Only a "climate emergency" would justify them. Investors were looking for quick gains in soon to be profitable industries. Wealthy international billionaires saw an opportunity for something worthwhile to do with their money that would make them feel good. They were "saving the planet". All this came together in Germany in the most expensive political and economic debacle of the century — and the planet was not saved.

The experience in Germany showed us the high environmental, economic, and social cost of using the wrong way forward on reducing CO_2 emissions. Darwell explains how the Nazi party had an historic anti-industrialist fixation on nature.[60] Foresters have the status of doctors in Germany. Hitler even built a huge windmill as an experimental source of power.

> *"After his denazification, the German philosopher, Martin Heidegger, preached anti industrial, environmental metaphysics. Marxist intellectuals from the Frankfurt School returned from exile in the U.S., where they had developed the New Left's synthesis of Marxism and environmentalism and sprouted their anti-democratic anti-rationalism across American universities."[61]*

Then they spread their pro-environment and anti-industrial philosophy through the universities and into the civil service and public using Nazi word manipulation techniques.

> *"The Frankfurt School had perfected the technique of taking two words with antithetical meaning and ramming them together to drain them of positive attributes."[62]*

This debating trick enabled activists to argue with phrases that nobody understood but sounded plausible enough to confuse and convince the casual listener — i.e., "climate change denier."

The Nazis had perfected the dark art of bullying, confusing and manipulating voters under Hitler. "Nazi storm troopers began as a security detail clearing the halls of Hitler's opponents during his rallies."[63] They also perfected the silencing of opposition through the endless repeating of the claim of Jewish responsibility for Germany's defeat in the First World War until it became accepted as true — as in the modern label, "climate change denier". These are the same techniques Donald Trump successfully used to avoid civil debate and silence his opponents in America — "lock her up"! This is how truth, freedom and democracy are being replaced by lies and a totalitarian elite as the silent majority sleeps.

In 1998, Germany's Red-Green coalition swept to power and began introducing the green revolution with subsidies for solar and wind power, including a 100,000 solar-roofs program with a €510 million grant. Angela Merkel inherited a bureaucracy riddled with Frankfurt graduates in senior government positions, who provided the "scientific" evidence for a major green revolution. A survey in May 1969 had found that 30% of West Germany's high-school and university students claimed to sympathize with Marxism or Communism.[64] The 2000 Renewable Energy Act was passed with minimal debate. It promised 100,000 clean energy jobs, an industrial boom and a 20% reduction in CO_2 emissions.

The 2010 *"Energiewend"* revolution included speeding up the shutting down of coal and nuclear power plants and massive subsidies for new wind and solar power companies. In 2004 the cost of this energy transformation was officially estimated at about €1 per household per month.

The consequences were devastating. Darwell observes that the 100,000 jobs went to China, and there were instead "...100,000 profiteers and a gigantic solar industry in China."[65] "In 2015 cumulative feed-in subsidies…the accrued cost of *Energiewend* had reached 4 billion euros." The tariff scheme, which paid $0.60 per KWH for solar power vs. $0.09 for small hydro projects and cost consumers 304 billion dollars. It destroyed the German power market and led to three German utilities companies losing €70 billion.[66] The poor have been devastated as electricity prices in Germany soared. "In 2012, thanks mainly to the headlong rush into wind and solar, Danes paid four times and Germans three and a half times what America did for their electricity."[67]

During this time, from 1999 to 2012, CO_2 emissions from German power stations rose by 17.2 million tons, or five percent.[68] This was clearly the wrong way forward. It was a step backward, because so much money was wasted on subsidies for wind and solar "rent seekers" in the uneconomic and inefficient wind and solar industries. This money would better have been invested in reactivating and developing nuclear power, the only proven adequate source for the massive power demands of modern society. This is what France did, and their CO_2 emissions went down.

The bad news is that the German climate disaster was exported to North America. The California experience mirrors that of Germany. The Frankfurt School exported its New Left Marxist anti-industrial ideology and political manipulation tactics to California. They built a similar coalition of New Left Marxist students, environmental activists with idealistic billionaires as backers. Environmentalism became the new religion of America and the Democratic Party.

As in Germany, wind and solar power was subsidized and mandated. The California power market was destroyed. Sixty-six percent of its industrial jobs disappeared. Generating capacity decreased by nine percent between 2002 and 2014, while demand rose by twenty-seven percent. The average monthly power bill increased by \$250.00 in coastal areas, where the wealthy live, and by \$500.00 inland, where ninety-nine percent of the population live.[69]

As in Germany, nuclear and large hydro power were excluded from the California Global Energy Solutions Act of 2006. The New Left Marxist agenda was shutting down the oil and gas industry and enriching the environment lobbyists and billionaires behind the new wind and solar plants. It was not about CO_2 reduction. Darwell goes into detail in explaining the political manipulation in California, which extended to the Obama Administration and Trudeau Government in Canada. U.S. NGOs and environmental foundations are still funding protests against Canadian pipelines to "fight climate change" (and keep American oil and natural gas prices high). Darwell names individuals and environmental NGOs and documents their multi-million-dollar international funding transfers.

Sadly, Obama went the same wrong way as Germany, promising 15 billion dollars a year to unprofitable wind and solar companies and green energy.[70] The heavily subsidized feed-in tariffs for wind and solar power in his 2015 Clean Power Plan cost between \$5.1 and \$8.4 billion.[71] The factor that Obama ignored in his plan, and the environmentalists opposed, was that the greener natural gas generated power from fracking was the real cause of emission reductions (from coal) in the US.

4.9: Challenging False Climate Science

We have met the enemy, and he is us.

—Walt Kelly (*Pogo*)

To challenge the fraud of false climate science the silent majority needs to know the truth. Many do but have been cowed into silence by activist's media bullying. The good news is that not everyone in Europe was fooled by the New Left Marxist/green socialist coalition. France for example, went the best right way currently available — nuclear. Today seventy percent of France's power is from nuclear plants. CO_2 emissions per-capita were 4.81 tonnes, compared with 9.12 tonnes in Germany in 2019.[72] Gross CO_2 emissions for France have decreased by thirty-two percent, from 408 tonnes in 2005 to 314 tonnes in 2019 (not that this affected global warming).

Climate Emergency is an example of Human Reason as False Truth. If we can recover the foundation of supernatural spiritual truths the fear of divine judgement will keep us a little more honest. Truth, freedom and democracy are worth fighting for.

5: Feminism as False Female

Many women are confused about their identity, depressed, and don't know who or what they are. Many are living in dysfunctional relationships or marriages that are unable to nurture children who will thrive as adults. Women have been devalued and lost their self-esteem and sexual identity to the false truths of a tiny sexually confused minority who don't know who or what they are.

Extreme feminism hijacked the original feminist goal of equal political rights with men. They redefined female to equal abilities or sameness as men, to compete for higher status or more interesting jobs in business and the professions. This liberation from tradition has been a blessing for the many women who were successful in competing with men for better paying, higher status or more interesting work. But this liberation has also devalued and confused the many other women who either could not compete successfully against men or chose to develop their natural intuitive, passive, and nurturing feminine gifts for marriage and family.

The many women who have achieved success in business, trades and the professions have had to pay a price. To compete with men, they have had to give up their traditionally more passive lifestyle for a more (manly) active, aggressive, and stressful life. While this redefinition of sameness of gifts and abilities as male was probably true for some women it was not true for most women. The extreme feminists were the different ones. We will examine the objective truths of the Bible, biology, physiology, psychology, marriage, and child rearing to see how these all agree that there is a unique female identity that is the opposite of, interdependent on and complementary to the male identity. Modern "same as men" woke feminism is a false and destructive definition of female.

Our examination of Biblical, physiological, biological, and psychological truth will show that sexual identity is binary. The truth of binary sexual identity is being very successfully and forcefully (no respectfulness there); redefined by many woke LGBTQ activists and imposed on the majority. These activists are the different ones. They are a tiny minority (said to be about 3%) who are so confused about their differentness they continue to add new definitions of a sexual identity of a smaller and smaller number of individuals. They are all lobbying for recognition and equal status as female or male. This is tragic. As we will see it is tragic for the LGBTQ community as they have disabled and silenced the only people who could help them live fuller richer lives — psychologists and those with the gift of Christian healing ministry. It's also tragic for many women who live impoverished lives because they have had their sexual identity hijacked and don't know who or what they are.

What is sexual identity for? In a word, as we will see in our review of biblical, biological, physiological, and psychological truth — reproduction of the species. While this may be uncomfortable, and not acceptable to feminist and LGBTQ activists, I am trying to help them find the truth — and set them (and all men and women) free.

Truth is what has been true for many people in many places and times; and what cannot be proven untrue. The false truths of feminism and the LGBTQ activists have been proven to be untrue. I am simply assembling the research. Nobody in a free democracy has the right to impose their understanding of truth on others. That is totalitarianism and the end of freedom and democracy.

The challenge is to recover feminine intuitive spiritual thinking, nurturing, and thriving marriages. We will propose compromises on marriage, abortion and conversion therapy legislation that would affirm all men and women in their sexual identity.

5.1: The Biblical Truth of Female

Most people in our Western culture are unaware of the rich wisdom teachings in the Bible from the creation story to Jesus. These teachings liberated women from ancient male domination and made them of equal value as persons and co-creators in the eyes of God. The ancient wisdom stories explain God's order of creation, the male-female relationship and our purpose as co-creators and rulers over creation. We will see that the first man was described as possibly androgynous (male and female) to emphasize the interdependence of male and female. The man was then intentionally divided into male and female. The point is that male and female are incomplete without the other. The Bible is often not about science but about spiritual wisdom. This story (not history) also teaches us that the glory and holiness of God is revealed in the self-sacrificial love relationship and union of the interdependent but opposite male and female. If we can grasp that God is love, this makes awesome sense!

Jewish and Christian teaching on women valued and honoured them equally with men. Many Protestants have not grasped the truth that Mary (possibly as a teenager) is honoured as the ideal Christian believer because she was in an intimate, dangerous, and self-sacrificial love relationship with God, and completely surrendered her life and will to God. Mary was "all-in" as a model believer.

Women are included among the leaders and heroes in Jewish history. Esther risked her life as Queen of Persia during the exile to save her people from extermination.

The Genesis Creation stories are divine wisdom teachings, revealed by the Holy Spirit. They explain the origin, nature, and destiny of mankind. Darwin explained how God created life on earth through the process of evolution, slight variations, and the survival of the fittest. Darwin's biological evidence includes the same biblical order of five discrete creation acts as the Bible. Darwin did not disprove the Bible. Darwin explained how God created a world that continues to become more perfect:

> *"Then God said, "let us make mankind in our image, in our likeness, so that they may rule over the fish in the sea and the birds in the sky, over the livestock and all wild animals, and over all the creatures that move along the ground." So, God created mankind in his own image, in the image of God he created them; male and female he created them."*
>
> *Genesis 1.26–27*

This may not be exactly what your Bible says because my New International Version is a 2013 revision by international scholars. Notice there is no "man," "women" or "him." There is also no hierarchy. "They" are made in God's image and "they" rule over creation. The second creation story helps us understand the relationship:

> *"Then the Lord God formed a man from the dust of the ground and breathed into his nostrils the breath of life, and the man became a*

living being.... But for Adam no suitable helper was found. So, the Lord caused the man to fall into a deep sleep; and while he was sleeping, He took one of the man's ribs and then closed up the place with flesh. Then the Lord God made a woman from the rib he had taken out of the man, and He brought her to the man. The man said "this is now bone of my bone and flesh of my flesh; she will be called woman for she was taken out of man. That is why a man leaves his father and mother and is united to his wife, and they become one flesh."

Genesis 2.7, 18, 20–24

There is no "my body" in a Jewish or Christian marriage. Woman is described as the "helper" which might offend feminists. But "helper" is not necessarily about status if you see this as an equal and interdependent relationship. Women help men (nourishment, bearing and caring for children). Men help women (protection, food, shelter). The important point is that man and woman were created as opposite and interdependent halves of a creative union. The point is not about status but about relationship.

God had to create male and female to ensure the continuation of the species. Darwin's theory of evolution, which some see as threatening Christianity, is a brilliant explanation of how God created everything so it could continue to evolve and become more glorious. Darwin brings science and the Bible together as truth. This divine order of creation is one of our seven lost spiritual truths. Darwin explained that as plants, animals and humans reproduce there are small variations. Some of these are progressive, others regressive. For example, fish that evolved their fins into wings and could fly could escape predators. Apes that evolved opposable thumbs could hold things like spears and protect themselves.

Being different is not a failure or a mistake. It just is. Denying being different is a mistake. Other people are confused. Affirming you in your differentness would be offensive. Affirming you as not different would be an obvious lie and denial of your unique gifts and who you are. You are stuck in a delusion, and nobody can help you deal with it. Evolutionary differences may or may not make us more fit to survive and have thriving children. Evolution and the survival of the fittest is how God's order of creation works to make creation more diverse, better, and more glorious. This is why it is natural and critical that men and women choose the most fit partner and raise more thriving children.

Jewish and Christian marriage is a spiritual union first and a sexual union second. Like many men who are not aware of the spiritual dimension, I learned this the hard way. The good news is that I did find a spiritual union the second time. I also discovered how things work in the spiritual dimension and have been blessed with 43 years of love, joy, thriving children and grandchildren.

In *Going Spiritual* I shared a healing ministry experience where in prayer, a man and I could both see the spiritual cords linking him to all the women he had had sexual relationships with. All his spiritual garbage could flow into them and theirs into him.[73] It was no wonder he was an alcoholic doing a Fourth Step confession. After much prayer, repentance, Confession and Absolution, The Holy Spirit showed me a spiritual sword to sever the chords. We could both see it going around the circle severing the cords. Finally, I prayed the precious blood of Jesus over the wounds to seal and heal them. This set the man free from his bondage. The man's face changed. He radiated joy and almost floated out the door in his new freedom. Sadly, most clergy have probably never had this basic teaching on sexual relationships and healing ministry. This was the "why" that young men and women need to hear about pre-marital sexual relationships in counselling. We all need to know the why behind the don't. Spiritual ignorance is not bliss — it is hell. This is the high cost of losing supernatural spiritual truth in the church.

This is why adultery is included in the Ten Commandments. The Commandments define what the Hebrews were to do as their part of the covenant relationship with God. Adultery is considered as serious as murder and was technically punishable under Hebrew law by stoning to death. As mentioned in Section 3.2, the reason Mary rode a donkey 90 km to Bethlehem — a life-threatening ride for a pregnant woman — was **not** so she could be registered. Only the men had to register their families. Behind the cute story is the likelihood she might be killed by the family. Nobody believed that God, not Joseph, was the father of the child. She was betrothed but not yet married to Joseph.

Many men and women do not find and fall in love with a marriage partner. Some find a more joyful spiritual love relationships with God, Jesus, the Holy Spirit, or saints such as Mary. This love nourishes their spiritual lives and gives them meaning and purpose as signs of God's glory in the world. This is part of the awesome diversity of God's glory and blessing.

In the New Testament God comes to earth as the divine/human Jesus, destined to teach and model self-sacrificial love and obedience by giving up His life as a sacrifice for the sins of the world. Instead of just teaching rules like the Pharisees, Jesus demonstrated how to pray for supernatural physical healing and take authority of oppressive demonic spirits and cast them out. In the first episode of the TV series, *The Chosen*, the leading Pharisee, Nicodemus, flees in terror when he tries to exorcise a demon tormenting a prostitute who attacks him. The next night we see her confused, disheveled, and stumbling around in the dark. A mysterious stranger calls her by name — Mary, she turns around as the stranger comes to her. He lays His hands on her head and frees her from the tormenting demons. The next day we see her again as the confident, radiant, and joy-filled Mary Magdalene walking through the city streets. When asked who the stranger was, she says, "I don't know but he said I belong to him." She is in a deep spiritual love relationship with Jesus — possibly the first Christian. She has been freed from her life of sin, made holy and received the spiritual gifts of love, joy and peace.

Women tend to understand the supernatural spiritual dimension more easily than men because they are naturally intuitive thinkers. They just know things. They don't know how or why they know them. Intuitive thinking is also essential for determining truth. The most reliable truth is when feminine intuitive thinking or knowing agrees with the male rational thinking or knowing. The devaluation of feminine intuitive and spiritual thinking and the supernatural dimension is the root cause of our social, moral, and political chaos.

The story of Jesus staying with the sisters Martha and Mary specifically honour two aspects of the feminine — Martha is the nurturer who prepares the food. Mary is the mystical intuitive who listens to and appreciates Jesus' teachings. (Luke 10.38–41)

The Apostle Paul defined the relationship between husband and wife as:

> *"The wife does not have authority over her own body but yields it to her husband. In the same way, the husband does not have authority over his own body but yields it to his wife.*

(1 Cor. 7:4–5)

Husbands are admonished to "love your wives, just as Christ loved the church and gave Himself up for her..." and "love their wives as their own bodies. He who loves his wife loves himself." (Ephesians 5.25, 28) This is about as valued and equal as female can get. This is the Judeo-Christian feminine — equal in value in the eyes of God and man. She is gifted with intuitive intelligence, business skills, family nurturer, parent, teacher and spiritually connected as co-creator of human life and nurturer. This is the biblical truth of feminine.

5.2: The Physiological, Biological and Psychological Truth of Female

Psychologist Karl Stein published his classic *The Flight from Women* in 1965 at the height of the feminist movement. Stein brings the gift of male rational thinking and professional psychological research into the debate begun by French philosopher Simone de Beauvoir's *The Second Sex* (1949). This debate was continued by Greer Garson's *The Female Eunuch* in 1970. Both were frustrated by the traditional role of women as stay-at-home wives and mothers. They sought to escape into what they saw as the more interesting, prestigious, and creative work of men. Stern concludes:

*"...the final result of Beauvoir's thesis is an
extraordinary impoverishment. What began
in feminism as a movement of liberation is*

Stern observes female physiology, and psychological nature is the opposite of male physiology and psychology. In general terms, women tend to work passively with nature (monthly periods, nine months bearing children). Stern observed that women who have abortions often tend to go into grief not after the abortion, but after the time when the child would normally have been born. He describes women who idolize men, are aggressive and reject love, dependence, and passivity as "phallic women." In contrast men tend to work more actively against nature (digging, cutting down, farming and building).[75]

Stein observes the importance of physiology in defining the feminine. "Her uniqueness, that which distinguishes her from man, lies in the biological."[76]

> *"Just as in the sexual physiology the female principle, is one of receiving, keeping and nourishing — woman's specific form of creativeness, that of motherhood, is tied to the life of nature, with a non-reflective bios.*"[77]

This physiological difference leads naturally to the nurturing, intuitive and mystical uniqueness of the female. Stein cites research by Erickson in 1951 that determined:

> *".... From experimental observations of the playing of pre-adolescent children that there are two distinct psychological trends that are determined primarily biologically and only secondarily by the child's expectation of its social role....the tendencies governing these*

constructions (i.e. buildings and scenes made out of toy materials) closely paralleled the morphology of the sex organs: in the male erectable and intrusive in character, serving highly mobile sperm cells; internal organs in the female, with vestibular access, leading directly to a statically expectant ova"[78]

The most obvious physiology is the concave female vagina clearly designed for the convex male penis.[79] This is consistent with the Creation story of human completeness in male — female unity. Stern extrapolated from Erickson and this physical evidence to explain the psychological feminine identity as generally "receiving" in contrast to the male identity as "penetrating." Men tend to be more active and "penetrate" the earth to farm and to build. Women are more receiving and passive in receiving sperm, bearing, and nurturing children. Men actively give sperm which women receive. This intimate uniting gives both men and women intense pleasure, emotional release, comfort, and the spiritual joy of love.

The strongest emotional drive in both men and women is for this physical and emotional unity and release. Sexual unity can lead to childbearing. Here again the physiology determines the female identity and need for unity with the male. The woman has breasts which are designed to both nourish children and to arouse sexual desire in men. Women and men both need the nourishment of this emotional love, unity, and physical passion.

When women are pregnant or nursing children, they need protection. They cannot easily run away and escape. They need men to protect them. This is perhaps the most important distinction between men and women. When my daughter Mary was born — I suddenly realized that now I was a "protector of women." One of the main reasons so many marriages fail in our time is that men do not realize that a woman's most basic need is for emotional affirmation and protection. Men need emotional affirmation and sexual intimacy. (Never make fun of your husband or wife!)

The biological need for nurturing children in utero and after birth requires non-verbal communication. The mother can intuitively sense trouble if something is wrong. The child is born sensing whether this is a safe place. Babies abandoned by their mothers and not held by nurses have died in hospitals. Before they can speak, babies can sense safety and love. For the same reason both children and animals will go to one person but not another in a crowded room. This is intuitive intelligence at work. It is a female and child survival skill. Female survival has always depended on knowing who really loves them and who will protect them.

Female intuitive thinking is the opposite of male rational thinking. Female intuitive thinking seems irrational to men because it is based on assembling information into a pattern intuitively. Women may or may not know how it is that they know something. They just know. In contrast male rational thinking disassembles information and analyzes it logically to find a pattern.[80] Stern describes female thinking as trans-rational. It goes beyond the physical and observable or scientific thinking to include the mysterious and metaphysical or spiritual. Stern's point is that to discern truth and real wisdom you need both rational thinking and intuitive thinking. This is why male rationalism and female intuition working together can generally come up with better answers than either male rationalism or female intuition working independently. It is also why our post-truth culture has lost authentic truth by depending on the male rationalism of scientific logic and disregarding the female intuitive, mystical, and poetic thinking.

Intuitive thinking is a mystical process — like reading poetry or prayer, where new words or ideas just float into consciousness. People reading a book or looking at a famous painting might suddenly see something they had not noticed or understood before. Religious men and women who have developed their intuitive or spiritual intelligence begin to understand how the supernatural dimension described in the Bible works. They may know intuitively that these words are authentic truth and wisdom. They may know intuitively that the great truths of the Bible are divinely inspired absolute truth. This is the opposite of flawed rational and politicized scientific truths post-truth our culture is now built on.

Stern is concerned about where this devaluation of intuitive thinking is leading. He quotes the concern of C.S. Lewis that:

> *"...the devaluation of poetic truth leads to a society in which a small minority of men will run mankind as if it were a compound of so many objects."*[81]

As a psychologist he is concerned that:

> *"The most striking and dramatic aspect of the psychoanalytic method is that metaphysics seems to be reduced to psychological mechanisms."*[82]

This has certainly been my experience as an Anglican priest in thirty years of healing and deliverance ministry. It began in seminary where we were not taught how to pray for the healing of sick and spiritually oppressed people. In the Bible, Jesus spent half of His time healing people supernaturally. I was rebuked in my pastoral care course for presuming that my prayers would move God to heal a child. I was asked to put a sheet over a doll in class and show the class how I would pray. Pastoral care has "evolved" from the healing and deliverance ministry of Jesus to providing non-denominational psychological listening, empathy, and encouragement.

In my Clinical and Pastoral Education course in Toronto we were sadly taught woke psychology — how to listen empathetically to hospital patients and offer words of comfort and encouragement. My training in healing and deliverance ministry was personal Bible study, prayer, workshops, lectures, books, and experience after seminary.[83] I realized that psychology — the study of the psyche or soul, had almost completely replaced priests and pastors in the role of "doctor of souls." The science of psychology is very helpful in the diagnosis of problems and advising people on how to cope with mental illness. Psychology is less successful in changing or healing people than Christian healing prayer ministry. Psychology is a soft science, based on evidence and reason that sadly excludes belief in the Holy Spirit as guide and healer. Non-Christian psychologists would also generally reject the idea of Satan, spiritual temptation, and spiritual oppression. My point is that there is just as much, if not more, physical evidence of both physical and spiritual healing through prayer ministry in many places and times. The world has not changed. Our definition of truth has changed.

5.3: Recovering Feminine Intuitive Spiritual Thinking

In Chapter 2: Human Reason as False Truth" and Chapter 3: Liberalism as False Christianity," we traced the devaluation of the supernatural and feminine intuitive mystical thinking as the Church leadership passed to men who had not experienced the guidance of the Holy Spirit, supernatural healing, and deliverance ministry. In our own time extreme woke liberals, feminists and LGBTQ activists have dismissed the supernatural in the Bible completely as mythical or prescientific superstition. As we have seen, the Bible directly contradicted them on male and female identity, purpose, and relationships.

Both evangelical and liberal church leaders have failed to defend the supernatural truths of Christianity. Instead, they tried the coward's way out of compromise, in the deluded hope of making the Church more relevant to society. This devalued intuitive mystical female thinking, the supernatural worldview of the Bible and the spiritual foundation of truth Western freedom and democracy rest on. The loss of the spiritual truths of the Bible in the culture has devalued the feminine intuitive and severely weakened the credibility and relevance of Christian churches.

There is a great hunger for spiritual truth and wisdom. Jordan Peterson's *12 Rules for Life* and *12 More Rules* and all his teachings are being devoured by millions of young people worldwide. They are looking for truth. He is doing from an intellectual and psychological perspective what most church leaders have failed to do. Peterson's Rule #4 in *Beyond Order* is, "Notice that opportunity lurks where responsibility has been abdicated." He has noticed the failure of the Church to teach the intuitive spiritual truths that affect our lives. He has explained how things work in the life inner life of the soul — and the consequences of human behaviour. Thousands of people flock to hear him around the world while churches are emptying. If you feed them, they will come.

The good news is that Jesus and the Holy Spirit are raising up new church leaders and new thriving churches that do teach the relevant spiritual truths of the Bible. The worldwide Anglican Communion has split in half. In the United Kingdom, a revival is underway. The Alpha Course-based New Wine Anglican churches are exploding with capacity crowds and massive outreach. They are filling huge ancient but abandoned churches. Leaders in declining churches need to check out Holy Trinity Brompton in London (htb.org). The (more orthodox) Anglican Church in North America says that it is planting a new church every 10 days.

Recovering and valuing feminine intuitive spiritual thinking in churches, schools and universities is the key to recovering truth, freedom, and democracy. If we do not value feminine intuitive thinking, we cannot value or understand how the supernatural dimension works. Intuitive thinking is an experience. Without personal experience of the supernatural we may know about, but cannot really understand, believe, and respect numinous truth. We are like the ancient Pharisees who knew the Law of God in their heads. But they did not know God. This focus on intellectual knowing blocked them and the modern Christian teachers who followed them, from loving God, listening with their hearts, and really hearing what God was saying. We need to recover feminine intuitive spiritual thinking to know God.

This devaluation of female intuitive spiritual thinking is why men and women have difficulty understanding each other. This is why we have so many failed marriages and divorces. This is why we need to defund school boards, colleges and universities that fail to teach the essential objective spiritual and psychological truths about women, men and the divine. Our freedom and thriving democracy depend on this.

5.4: Recovering Child Nurturing and Marriage

> *"In a word, nuptial love indicates the total gift of self...rests on three interrelated dynamics: the complementarity of sexual differences or otherness; the call to communion through the self-giving love to which these summonses us; and the fecundity to which this communion leads."*
>
> Pope John Paul II,
> *Homily on the Feast of the Holy Family,*
> *December 30, 1988, p. 12.*

Marriage and families have always been and still are the building blocks of a society and a nation. Judeo-Christian marriage is a spiritual male-female union in "Holy Matrimony." It is not a partnership or purely legal arrangement. It is the joining (physically and spiritually) of the opposite but interdependent male and female. The two become one. There is no more "my way" or "my body." It becomes "our way," and "our bodies." This involves the self-sacrificial *"agape"* (αγάπη) love, unique to the Greek of the Christian New Testament. This love includes self-sacrifice, forgiveness, more forgiveness, patience, and kindness. When the love, forgiveness and spiritual bond is broken or betrayed, the marriage unity ends and the family shatters into psychological pain, suffering and poverty. The Apostle Paul says it best:

1 Corinthians 13.4–7

This is very different from our pagan, more male and rational understanding of love as more physical, less spiritual; and sexual attraction more like the Greek *"eros"* or lust. Agape love is much more powerful than the way people casually say they love chocolate or love hockey.

The extreme feminist redefinition of women as the same as men has devalued feminine nurturing in male-female relationships and raising thriving future citizens. This has impoverished women and led to dysfunctional male-female relationships, families unable to raise thriving future citizens and huge social costs.

Feminism and the availability of effective birth control in the Sixties changed the dynamics of marriage. Women could now have more casual sexual relationships without risking the responsibility for bearing and raising children. This led to couples delaying marriage and child rearing to pursue higher education and more exciting careers in business and the professions.

Women were no longer as dependent on men for financial and emotional support. The rate of marriages declined from 900 per 100,000 in 1967 to 500 per 100,000 in 1997.[84] Financial and emotional independence also made divorce a more attractive option if the marriage was not satisfying. The divorce rate soared. In Canada the number of divorces soared from around 30,000 in 1970 to 100,000 in 1985. The numbers have since declined to around 45,000 in 2020, but this does not include statistics for breakups of the 21 % of marriages that were Common Law (2016).[85] Each of these family breakups has emotionally and financially devastated a family and the lives of men, women and mostly children — I speak from painful experience.

One of the most compelling arguments for saving the traditional Judeo-Christian marriage is the 1877 study of the "Jukes" family (a pseudonym to protect later descendants). It was done by New York prison authorities to establish the social and moral cost of one unmarried atheist couple over five generations.[86] In an exhaustive examination of county and state records researchers identified 700 of 1,200 known descendants. The five-generation study of the atheist, common-law "Jukes Family" study was published in 1875. It was updated in 1915 after Arthur Estabrook's original notes were found. The 1915 report updated the social cost to government with family data to 1915:

> *"In the present investigation, 2,820 people have been studied, inclusive of all considered by Dugdale; 2,094 were of Juke blood and 726 of 'X' blood who married into the Juke family; of these 366 were paupers, while 171 were criminals; and 10 lives have been sacrificed by murder. In schoolwork 62 did well, 288 did fairly, while 458 were retarded two or more years. It is known that 166 never attended school; the school data for the rest of the family were unobtainable. There were 282 intemperate (alcoholics) and 277 harlots. The total cost to the State has been estimated at $2,093,685."[87]*

This has been compared to study of the Jonathan Edwards family's five contemporary generations to the

Jukes in the U.S. The Christian Edwards family had no criminals or paupers, one vice-President, members of Congress, a senator, over 100 lawyers, 13 college presidents, 100 clergymen, and 129 graduates from Yale.[88]

The devastation of children's lives has been the greatest emotional and social cost of radical woke feminism. Children learn how to get along with the opposite sex and how to be a family from observing their parents. Multiple studies have consistently shown that:

> *"...children who grow up without the **continuous presence of both mother and father** are twice as likely to drop out of school as children raised by both biological parents...score lower on standardized tests, receive lower grades, are less likely to choose college..."*[89]

> *This in turn leads to lower paying jobs, lost economic potential, poverty, increased welfare costs, increased policing and justice costs and men and women without the social and communication skills to form a healthy family. The culture and the state cannot afford to indulge those who want to deny their differentness by claiming normal marriage status for their relationship.*

The way forward is to recover the truth and value of feminine nurturing by finding a compromise on legislation that protects and recognises the social value of male-female marriage.

In *Chapter 11: Recovering a Democratic Compromise*, I propose electing politicians who will challenge and revise marriage, human rights and anti-discrimination legislation that discriminates against the uniqueness of male-female relationships.

6. Homosexuality as False Male

"I was interrupted by a woman anxiously waving her hand for permission to be heard — 'I don't think anyone knows what male is?' she cried out. She is very nearly right."[90]

As this is a very important but controversial chapter, I beg my readers to withhold judgement until they have considered all the biblical, physiological, and psychological research presented. Freedom of speech and democracy depend on everyone having the right to respectfully share personal experiences, beliefs and what they have learned — and on nobody having the right to impose their beliefs on others. Minorities imposing their beliefs on the majority is the root cause of our loss of truth and the social chaos that is eroding our freedom of speech and democracy.

Homosexuality as false male is the other side of the identity crisis of feminism as false female. In both cases a small minority of men and women have a sexual orientation or personal characteristics that are the opposite of the norm for their biological identity. The issue is that instead of accepting their differentness from the norm and trying to adapt, they have politically imposed their different experience of the truth of male identity on the majority, who have a sexual orientation and characteristics that match their biological identity. As we will see the majority has been bullied and manipulated into accommodating the minority. This has meant giving up their understanding of the uniqueness of male identity. It's very confusing and demoralizing.

This has created a sexual identity crisis for both men and women and caused enormous social damage to marriages, families, and the nurturing of future citizens. As we have seen in the Chapter *5: Feminism as*

False Female, woke feminist LGBTQ activists created this chaos by pressuring opportunistic politicians into revising human rights legislation to prefer the rights of the minority over the majority rights of heterosexual married couples, more likely to nurture successful future citizens.

To understand this issue on a deeper level we need to move beyond simplistic debating points and examine the objective truths of the Bible, physiology, and psychology. This is critical, as much of the controversy and our social disorder are generated by those who are ignorant of or willfully ignoring the scientific evidence that contradict their understanding of sexual identity. We will see that the evidence of all three is consistent in saying homosexuality is a false or disordered male or female identity.

The male identity crisis is a crisis of truth. Men do not know who they are. They do not know how to relate to women. Many do not know what their role in society is or what men are supposed to do. My objective is to present the evidence fairly and propose a political compromise that will respect the dignity of all men and free them from the present crisis in masculinity which has been so destructive to men, marriage, children, and our social order.

6.1 The Psychological War on Masculinity

The men in our post-truth culture are confused. They do not know who they are and what is expected of them. In Chapter 5, we have seen how male identity has been devalued and stolen by activists re-defining female as being equal to male in the sense of all having the same gifts and abilities as men. Feminists needed this more masculine identity to compete for traditionally male positions. More damage was done when feminist activists politicized hiring practices by demanding affirmative action policies. The result has been that more qualified men were denied promotions or positions. This new woke culture of confused identity affirmation is destroying marriages, families, the education system, professions, and our competitiveness as a nation.

Gay and lesbian activists added to the confusion over male identity by also claiming to be just like other men (same gifts and abilities) and demanding equal status, recognition and benefits for same-sex partnerships, unions, and marriages. Their Gay Pride marches began as a way of drawing attention to the need for the legitimate recognition and affirmation of the gay and lesbian community. As in extreme feminism this quickly evolved into an aggressive political action group, demanding legal human rights protection from discrimination.

The war on masculinity began with the picketing of the American Psychiatric Association annual convention in 1973 until the leadership agreed to remove homosexuality from its official *Diagnostic and Statistical Manual of Mental Disorders*.[91] This was the culmination of years of internal professional disagreement. Freud advised a mother in 1935 that homosexuality was neither a vice, degradation or illness.[92] "...German physician Richard von Krafft-Ebing viewed the condition as pathological — that is a mental illness."[93] Sandor Rado viewed homosexuality as a mental illness produced by bad parenting — specifically an overbearing mother and a distant father.[94] Rocca quotes Edmond Burger, a leading psychoanalyst of the 1950s, writing "I have no bias against homosexuals; for me they are sick people requiring medical help." The First edition of the APS Diagnostic and Statistical Manual (DSM) classified homosexuality as a "sociopathic personality disturbance."

The crisis of male identity has now been embedded in human rights legislation through the politicized and unprofessional support of the American Psychiatric Association. Their agreement to remove homosexuality/sexual dysphoria (confusion) from the DSM to end activist picketing of their national convention is accepted as "scientific proof" that homosexuality is normal male behaviour. The consequence has been the intimidation and silencing of opposing voices in the psychology profession. This is a denial of professional responsibility and free speech.

This professional intimidation and in effect denial of freedom of speech is now enforced by human rights tribunals composed of activists with no legal or professional training. These tribunals operate outside the normal judicial system and its assumption of innocence until proven guilty. Instead, the party charged must defend themselves and prove their innocence at their own expense. The expenses of the complainant are often funded by the tribunal. Human rights tribunals have evolved way beyond their original good intention of preventing unfair racial discrimination into a tool of intimidation against free speech. These tribunals need to be abolished or brought under the rules of the criminal judicial system.

In 2019 the APA issued its new *"Guidelines for Psychological Practice with Boys and Men."* This has generated a storm of protest from respected professionals including Jordan Peterson who calls the *Guidelines* "...an all-out assault on masculinity...":[95]

> *"The coup of the APA undertaken by the ideologues is now complete. The field has been compromised, perhaps fatally. And the damnable Guidelines provide sufficient, but no means exhaustive evidence of that."*

"We cannot allow ideology and political correctness to prevail over science. The Boys and Men document is propagandistic to a degree that is almost incomprehensible."

"There is also no agreement that gender exists solely in the form of "roles" that are learned (as opposed to innate) — although all reasonable scientists agree that much of human behaviour, including that related to sex, is learned."

Peterson exposes the misguided and unscientific anti-masculine bias of the authors. For example, the statement that: "socialization for conforming to traditional masculinity has been shown to limit males' psychological development, constrain their behaviour, result in gender role strain and gender conflict, and negatively influence mental health" is the opposite of the evidence-based truth of most clinical psychological experience. He notes these traits are based primarily on the very limited research of the four authors of the *Guidelines*. Peterson warns that this creeping politicization has led to a de-emphasis on real science in training psychologists. This has seriously eroded the ability of psychologists to provide the best care possible to clients.

Author Christine Rosen echoes Peterson in her article, "The Psychological War on Masculinity."[96] She also shows how the *Guidelines* focus on attacking and deconstructing masculinity as a psychological problem. This is contrary to the evidence of male psychological issues of our time that show "drug use, high suicide rates, educational achievement that lag far behind that of women and shortened life expectancy."[97]

Restoring the truth of masculinity, male identity and male confidence is the psychological solution to recovering the truth of masculinity. It is not the psychological problem. These signs of social chaos and dysfunction are all signs that men are confused about their identity and purpose in life. Rosen describes the supposedly professional quality research the new guidelines are based on as full of vague jargon and sounding more like:

> *"...a term paper written by a mediocre woman's studies major...and heavily biased against masculine characteristics, which are asserted (without proof) to be harmful and which psychologists are urged to quash".*[98]

This is the heart of the problem. Boys are failing in schools because their traditionally masculine behaviour such as the competitiveness of high achievers is being discouraged. They are taught by their mostly female teachers that masculinity is a disruptive disorder. Rosen concludes:

> *"Left-leaning psychologists might not like the men who embody stoicism, or the competitive instinct that fuels high achievers, or the disciplined aggression that makes for an ideal soldier, but our world would be a less free and prosperous place without them."*[99]

In the sections below on psychological truth and Judeo-Christian Truth, we will see that men do have innate traits. Boys need an affirming, loving, gentle father, to help them grow into their male identity, have positive relationships with women and better mental health. There is an overwhelming consensus that the lack of an affirming father is the most common cause of sexual dysphoria.

The LGBTQ activists' victory over the psychological profession has made them feel comfortable in their false gender identity. But it has confused men and robbed them of their unique identity, meaning and purpose in life. The activists have used this "professional" approval of their false identity to push leftist politicians into passing human rights, hate speech and conversion therapy legislation that potentially criminalizes those who question the truth of gender dysphoria being a normal male condition.

The LGBTQ activists also realized that if psychological counselling or Christian prayer ministry could help men and women recover their birth identity, this would be irrefutable evidence that sexual dysphoria was a disorder and not normal. Something that can be cured, healed, or fixed is not normal.

Gay and lesbian activists have now set up a perfect support system to protect their false truth. They have silenced criticism and continue to redefine gender. They have infiltrated the school system and gained the support of well-intentioned teachers. They could freely encourage young adolescent children to explore alternative gender identities. The state would give them free (politicized) psychological and medical help in changing from birth gender to the opposite gender to see if it was more comfortable.

This is the problem. According to a psychologist of my acquaintance, over half of young adolescents who transitioned medically and surgically into a non-birth sexual identity, became disillusioned later as adults. Some sought out and found psychological, spiritual, and medical help in transitioning back to their birth gender. Red lights flashed on with the transgender lobbyists. They saw the huge threat to their lie of normality and non-brokenness.

Sadly, a very small number of reprehensible, unprofessional, and un-Christian pastors had tried to bully, brainwash, and forcibly convert adolescents back to their birth gender. This handful of abusive forced gender conversions by evangelical pastors was publicized by trans activists and used to justify anti-conversion therapy legislation (Bill C-6 in Canada, 2021). It is a very confusing piece of legislation. An opportunistic leftist majority in Parliament passed a poorly drafted law which included contradictory statements that:

- Conversion therapy doesn't work.
- Criminalized anyone involved in conversion therapy (back to birth gender only).
- Failed to distinguish between obviously criminal forced conversion therapy and voluntary conversion therapy by professionally trained psychologists and clergy.
- Criminalized Psychologists and professional clergy who even advertised their availability to offer professional counseling on transition to birth gender.

The overall effect of this law is that more than half of adolescents who convert from their birth gender as adolescents, and then change their mind as mature adults, cannot legally seek professional psychological or spiritual counselling on converting back to their birth gender in Canada. The Canadian conversion legislation is a one-way street that traps young people in a nonbirth gender. This is a destructive and discriminatory loss of personal and professional freedom of speech and counselling. It protects the LGBTQ communities right to transgender but robs those who transgender of the right to transgender back to birth identity.

Sadly, the education, psychology and medical professions have all failed to act responsibly and professionally. They have failed to develop guidelines that would protect vulnerable adolescents in schools from LGBTQ activists and naïve supporters. They have failed to protect sexually immature children from making premature and often tragic decisions about their sexual identity. It is time to challenge professionals to be less political and more professional as guardians of objective truth.

6.2 Biblical Truth of Male Identity

"Then you will know the truth, and the truth will set you free."

John 8.32

Our examination of the objective truth (true to all people in all times and places) begins with the Biblical truth about homosexuality and identity of men. This truth may surprise and offend some readers. I am going to quote what the Bible says. This may be different from what others may have told you it says. For political reasons activists as well as some priests and pastors, have sadly misrepresented what the Bible says. This has been shameful and very hurtful to the LGBTQ community. Many in the LGBTQ community are sensitive and devout Christians searching for a loving Christian community and a spiritual life of joy. Their faithfulness over centuries of Church persecution should be an example to us all. This persecution and conflict over biblical truth have been destructive to the faith of all believers and confusing to nonbelievers. It has powered the deconstruction of the Bible and Christianity by intellectuals, extreme liberals and woke activists. I speak as an ordained Anglican priest who knows and fears that we who teach will be judged most harshly by Jesus.

I am committed to speaking the truth in love and not judging others. My hope is that the truth will set all men and women free to grow and thrive in lives of dignity.

6.2.1: The Genesis Creation Stories (1.26–34; 2.4–25)

In "Feminism as False Female," we reviewed the Creation stories in Genesis (1.26–34 and 2.4–25) to understand the divine order and process of creation. We learned that the order of creation is hierarchical with men and women entrusted with the joint authority and joint responsibility for ruling over all creation. We also saw how the process of creation was evolution — small natural physical variations, some of which were more successful in ensuring survival, that ensured that creation gradually became more perfect as a sign of God's glory in the world. Women would compete for the strongest man who could impregnate them and support and protect them through the long process of childbearing and raising children. Men would seek the most attractive woman who could comfort and nurture them sexually and bear and raise their children. Marriage relationships were a love union of interdependent opposites. They were both equal "helpers."

After writing this in Chapter 5, I was blessed by a brother priest who said Pope John Paul II had said this in his encyclical *"Man and Woman He Created Them: A Theology of the Body"*:

> *"The image of God is found in man and woman above all in the communion of love between them, which reflects the communion of love between the persons of the Trinity (TOB 9:3). In God's design, the spousal union of man and woman is the original effective sign through which holiness entered the world.*

> *This visible sign of marriage "in the beginning" relates to the visible sign of Christ's spousal love for the Church and is thus the foundation of the whole sacramental order*
>
> *(TOB 95b:7)."*

In simple, non-theological language: male–female marriage is the most important part of the divine order of creation. This is how we are co-creators and able to fulfill our mandate to rule over creation. Those in the Church who have taken marriage casually are in very serious spiritual trouble.

In *Theology of the Body Explained,* Christopher West quotes John Paul saying: "In the entire world there is not a more perfect, more complete image of God, unity and community." And "In a word, nuptial love indicates the total gift of self…rests on three intellectual dynamics: the complementariness of sexual differences or 'otherness' the call to communion through self-giving love to which this summons us; and the fecundity to which this communion leads."[100]

All three of these truths have been lost in our post-Christian and post-truth culture. Individualism has replaced the interdependence of men and women. The "otherness" of the male-female relationship has been replaced by the "sameness" of feminism. The unity and community of self-giving love have been replaced by selfishness and "my way." Humanity has been greatly impoverished by the false gods of liberalism, feminism, and progressivism.

While male-female sexual relationships are the most fit in continuing the work of creation or norm, we must remember that the glory of creation is also in its diversity. Same-sex relationships are not most fit, but they are also a natural part of variations in the divine order of creation (evolution) and its consequence. In

Chapter 5, we saw that same-sex relationships have historically produced less successful future citizens than male-female relationships. So, while same-sex relationships work for some individuals and enrich their lives, they are to be celebrated but clearly differentiated from the more fit male-female norm. Just as God must give us freedom to reject His love, we must give each other the freedom to be different.

6.2.2: Sodom and Gomorrah (Genesis 19)

Abraham's brother Lot separates from him and settles as a foreigner in Sodom. When angels from God come to visit Lot, the men of Sodom gather outside Lot's house at night and demand he brings them out so (in Hebrew) "we can get to know them". This was traditionally interpreted as "have coitus with them." Lot pleads with them not to do this, refuses to bring the angels out and offers his virgin daughters as substitutes. The consequence was that despite Lot pleading for God to spare the town, he is warned to run away with his family and the Lord rains fire and brimstone on the town destroying it completely. This story teaches us the Hebrew consequence of dishonoring God and breaking the order of creation and the holiness covenant was spiritual and physical death. This is the origin of the word "sodomy."

Hebrew scholar Derrick Bailey gives us an alternative interpretation. He argues that the Hebrew word translated as "get to know" is more often interpreted in the Old Testament as "get to know about socially" and presents an alternative explanation for the town's hostility and destruction. [101] Apparently the people of Sodom were known and mentioned in the Old Testament for their lack of hospitality and hostility to strangers. Lot as a newcomer or stranger was apparently given hospitality but that had its limits. As a stranger he could not offer hospitality to newcomers. That was the prerogative of the men of the town. This interpretation would mean it would be natural that the men of the town would want to get to know Lot's visitors to see if they were friends, spies, or potential enemies.

Bailey also claims the homosexual interpretation is referenced more in the New Testament than Old, presumably because homosexuality was rampant in the pagan cultures surrounding Israel.[102] He explains the fire and brimstone story as possibly related to known bituminous and salt deposits in the area which could have caught fire and exploded.

I am not qualified to comment on Hebrew, but it seemed fair to include this as one scholar's opinion, a minority view. It does seem to be stretching the overall evidence, particularly Lot's offer of his virgin daughters as substitutes. This is where intellectualism can be the enemy of truth. Bailey's interpretation of scripture is based on reason alone. It may or may not have also been based on his personal experience. This is where human reason alone has led the LGBTQ community. Other than the medical and sanitary issues of sodomy, it does not seem immoral. Two people are giving each other comfort.

6.2.3: The Ten Commandments

The Bible is about having a holy spiritual relationship of love with God. God is holy. We are unholy. Holy means pure, whole, complete, and perfect. God's love is like a holy fire that consumes anything unholy in God's presence. This is the first of our seven spiritual truths that has been lost. This is why we need rules, like the Ten Commandments, to understand how to obey God and live a holy life that seems unreasonable to secular people.

The Ten Commandments given by God to Moses after the Exodus from Egypt (1290 BC), summarize the heart of the Judeo-Christian truth of God's order. This is the pre-Christian foundation of divine order that enabled the Hebrews to thrive and overcome their enemies for the last 3,000 years. The Ten Commandments define what the Hebrew people would do — love and obey God exclusively and love their neighbour as themselves. The Ten Commandments, which are the basis of our legal system, are the details or tests of our love of God and neighbour. The first five Commandments (summarized) are tests of our love of God:

1. You shall have no other gods.

2. You shall not make an image of anything and worship it.

3. You shall not misuse my name.

4. You shall observe the Sabbath day.

5. Honour your father and mother.

The second five commandments (summarized) are tests of our love of neighbour:

6. You shall not murder.

7. You shall not commit adultery.

8. You shall not steal.

9. You shall not give false witness.

10. You shall not covet (wrongly desire) anything that belongs to your neighbour.

These are all explained in detail in the Book of Deuteronomy.

Homosexuality is condemned in the holiness code of the book of Leviticus, which is an extended exposition of the Ten Commandments concerned with holiness and ritual:

> *18.22: "Do not have sexual relations with a man as one does with a woman; that is detestable."*
>
> *20.13: "If a man has sexual relations with a man as one does with a woman, both of them have done what is detestable. They are to be put to death; their blood will be on their own hands."*

There is little evidence this sentence was carried out very often. Leviticus in my mind is more a priestly intellectual interpretation or manual than an authentic word of divine revelation. Jesus for examples castigates the priests and Pharisees for laying impossible burdens on people's backs and focusing on procedure over love of God and neighbour. While homosexuality is not specifically mentioned in the Commandments, adultery is broadly interpreted as protecting the purity and holiness of sexual relationships within marriage. Homosexual practice would be a breach of this holiness and purity. It is also a rejection of the divine order of male-female marriage in creation.

6.2.4: New Testament Biblical Truth

The books of the New Testament of the Bible describe the life of Jesus and the first Century of the growth of the early Christian Church. It was written in Greek, starting about 30 years after the death and resurrection of Jesus in AD 32. The New Testament authenticates and rests on the truth foundation of the Old Testament scriptures. Jesus did not come to replace the Covenant of Moses (Ten Commandments) but to fulfill it.[103] "Do not think that I have come to abolish the Law or the Prophets; I have not come to abolish them but to fulfill them."

Jesus' teaching was an elaboration and extension to the Ten Commandments. Love was more clearly defined as self-sacrificial obedience and love ("*agape*" in Greek) of God and neighbour. Greek has five words for love including "*philios*" (i.e. Philadelphia the city of brotherly love) and "*eros*" (erotic love). Jesus demonstrated this self-sacrificial love by obeying Father God's will that he should die on a cross for the sins of the whole world. The Ten Commandments said husbands should not commit adultery. Jesus taught "Husbands, love your wives, just as Christ loved the church and gave himself up for her" (Ephesians 5.25).

For this reason, marriage or holy matrimony is considered a sacrament in Christian churches. A sacrament is an outward visible sign of an inward spiritual grace. The couple make outward promises and exchange rings. They are also bound together spiritually by their love and by the physical joining together of their bodies in matrimonial sex. I shared in *Going Spiritual* a healing experience where both I and the person being healed could see the silver cords linking him to all the women that he had had a sexual relationship with).[104]

Marriage is holy because it is a permanent spiritual as well as a legal relationship that is blessed by a priest. Jesus is considered the third party in Christian marriage. Sexual relationships within such a marriage are holy. In contrast if either the man or woman has a sexual relationship outside the marriage that is condemned as unholy and the sin of adultery — from "adulterate," to dilute or water down. Adultery was always considered as breaking a solemn promise of loyalty and a violation of the Ten Commandments.

The gay and lesbian community are correct when they say Jesus did not say anything about homosexuality. This does not mean He approved. It most likely meant everyone knew it was a forbidden practice.

The New Testament letters of the Apostle Paul, who was chosen and anointed by Jesus, do condemn homosexual acts as a form of sexual immorality:

> *Romans 1.27: "In the same way, the men also abandoned natural relations with women and were inflamed with lust for one another. Men committed shameful acts with other men and received in themselves the due penalty for their error."*

> *1 Cor. 6.9–10: "Or do you not know that wrongdoers will not inherit the kingdom of God? Do not be deceived: Neither the sexually immoral nor idolaters nor adulterers nor men who have sex with men nor thieves nor the greedy nor drunkards nor slanderers nor swindlers will inherit the kingdom of God.*

> *1 Tim. 1.9–10: "We also know that the law is made not for the righteous but for lawbreakers and rebels, the ungodly and sinful, the unholy and irreligious, for those who kill their fathers or mothers, for murderers, for the sexually immoral, for those practicing homosexuality, for slave traders and liars and perjurers—and for whatever else is contrary to the sound doctrine."*

6.2.5: Truth of Christian Healing Ministry

The Good News of Christianity is the forgiveness of sins, physical and spiritual healing, and the hope of an eternal spiritual life of joy in Jesus Christ. This Good news is sadly threatening to many woke LGBTQ activists. They would have to face their differentness and rebellion against God's order and come to Jesus for forgiveness and healing. This would be painful and traumatic. Tragically, they have chosen to deny and deconstruct the foundation of Judeo-Christian spiritual truth that could help them. They have completed the long, slow historical process of dismissing the supernatural truth of the Bible as mythical and superstition. Satan has used them and liberalized and intellectualized religious leaders to confuse, divide and destroy many of the churches Jesus died for. Healing and deliverance ministry has been lost in most Christian churches. The Good News is that God is not defeated. God has kept a remnant of mostly lay people who have continued this work, often outside the official church. The Good News in our time is that this ministry is being revived in some churches as the Holy Spirit raises up and anoints new leaders.

Healing and deliverance ministry is the evidence that proves homosexuality can be healed. Homosexuality is not a normal healthy male identity. While it may be normal for those in the homosexual community, it is not normal for most men and women. The original psychological term "sexual dysphoria" means confusion. Confusion can be faced and turned into order if the person desired this.

What I have learned about healing and deliverance ministry for gender confusion may upset and shock some readers, but this evidence of experience from divinely called and professionally qualified healing prayer ministers is central to my argument that homosexual practice is not normal male behaviour.

This vital Christian ministry has tragically been disgraced by the publicity around a few sensational and disgusting attempts at forced conversion by unqualified and un-Christian pastors. Forced conversion is impossible, destructive, un-Christian and illegal. The biblical (and Star Trek) prime directive is to respect personal/local freedom. If God wants us to have a genuine love relationship with Him, God must give us the freedom to choose to not love Him and walk away. Authentic Christian priests and pastors are bound by this principle and must wait until people come to them voluntarily for spiritual counselling or healing prayer ministry. Anything less would be religious and spiritual abuse.

While I do not have any personal experience in this ministry I have been to workshops where formerly gay men and lesbian women have shared the story of their conversion back to birth identity. My late mentor John L. Sandford and his wife Paula were pioneers in this ministry. In their bestselling book *Transformation of the Inner Man*, they devote a whole chapter to healing homosexuality.[105] They begin with a general warning to counsellors that this ministry must be voluntary, focused on loving the sinner but hating the sin, and may face vigorous opposition by the gay and lesbian community. This ministry is not for those without a deep faith, a divine call and gifting, professional training, experience in spiritual warfare and great courage.

Sandford explains that homosexuality, like alcoholism, can become a spiritual bondage. This is the spiritual "strong man" of the Bible who must be spiritually bound before deliverance and healing can start (Matthew 12.29). In the Bible, Jesus used examples from the physical world to explain how things work in the supernatural dimension. For example, the "strong man" Jesus is talking about is not a physical man but a strong demonic spirit. This spirit can mentally blind or imprison a person in a mental stronghold. They can physically hear those urging them to get help, but their minds automatically block this as foolish. It's a form of natural psychological self-deception working with the demonic. It's complicated. Fuller explanations are available in Sandfords' *Deliverance and Inner Healing* and my *Going Spiritual: Discovering, Developing and Healing a Spiritual Life*. If you have talked to a serious alcoholic, you have talked to someone in a mental stronghold. This is an area where Christian healing and deliverance ministry can be more effective than psychology.

The Sandfords' explain the most common cause of homosexuality as poor or absent fathering.

> *"In all of our years of counselling we have never found a homosexual or lesbian who had or related well to a strong, gentle, loving father."*[106]

Other causes mentioned include:

- Mothers who drive boys to reject becoming close to a woman.

- Fathers who reject emotional relationships with daughters.

- Fetuses sensing a boy or girl is strongly desired by parents and trying to please them by adopting opposite sex characteristics.

- Children born with physical manifestations that are both male and female (hermaphrodites).

- Tendency toward homosexuality may be inherited.

- Exposure to practicing sodomites at swimming pools or summer camps.

The Sandfords teach that healing prayer ministry must be voluntary. They encourage clients to seek professional psychological advice on coping mechanisms as a first step. Healing prayer ministry begins with in-depth counselling to find the root cause. If it was a lack of parenting, either John or Paula would spend extra time with the person as surrogate parents, modelling and affirming the person's birth gender as a strong, gentle, loving mother or father would have done. If the root cause was a sexual assault or rape the victim would be led in prayer through the confession, absolution, and healing process of forgiving the perpetrator and breaking the spiritual bondage of unforgiveness. If the person feels personal guilt that too is taken to the Cross of Jesus for confession, absolution, and healing.

John Sandford shares that in one case he had to ask the Holy Spirit for more guidance, go deeper in prayer to see a vision of the client's male and female poles physically crossed. He was given instructions to reach inside the person in prayer and disentangle the poles.[107] This prayer ministry and supportive counselling restored the client to his birth identity and manhood.

Like Sandford, Leanne Payne begins her prayer ministry by inviting the Holy Spirit to come and be part of the conversation as the client unpacks their story from birth to adulthood. She gently leads the person through the confession and absolution process to free them from the top layer of sin-guilt and shame. This conversation also exposes the root cause of the homosexuality and any trauma or unforgiveness associated with it.

One of my most important learnings has been how legalistic things are in the spiritual dimension. You would never think that a child who was assaulted or raped would have to forgive the perpetrator! But they do. Unforgiveness is a sin that connects a person spiritually to the perpetrator until it is confessed and taken to the Cross for forgiveness. This is where Christian prayer ministry can often help victims of trauma more effectively than secular psychology. Trauma is particularly dangerous spiritually. The memory of trauma may open a doorway for spiritual oppression that cannot be helped or "coped with" through psychological counselling.

The good news is that many people have been healed from gender confusion and restored to healthy sexual relationships with opposite gendered people. The bad news is that many churches in our time have been intellectualized, politicized, and dismissed the gifts of the Holy Spirit including healing and deliverance ministry as mythical. The tragic news is that because of a few forced gender conversions by untrained and unprofessional evangelical pastors, Canada has criminalized professional counselling and prayer ministry related to conversion therapy (back to birth gender only. Sadly, here are no restrictions on psychologists, doctors, teachers, activists, and counsellors encouraging vulnerable adolescents to explore changing from their birth gender in high school. We propose a compromise to improve this legislation and end a socially destructive denial of freedom and failure to protect children in schools in Chapter *9: Recovering Objective Truth.*

6.3: The Science of Male and Homosexuality

> *"...the homosexual man or woman is basically a man or woman by genetic determination and homosexually oriented by learned preference."*[108]

We will begin with the question "what is male?" as the other half of Carl Stern's description of male and female characteristics. Next, we will review the key question of whether male and female identities are primarily biologically determined or learned from experience. This brings us to the objective truth about the causes and treatment of homosexuality.

As we noted above in Feminism, Stern describes the male physiology as opposite to and complementary to the female identity:[109]

> *"The male convex penis is designed to penetrate the concave vagina. Natural conception requires multiple penetrations over many months which requires a longer-term relationship between the man and woman."*

> *"The powerful male sexual drive is aroused by female breasts which draw male and female together in an intimate relationship."*

> *"The male bone and muscle structure is better designed for running, fighting, attacking. This complements the female physiology designed for bearing and nurturing children, which cannot as easily run away and needs protection. Women are naturally attracted to strong men who can protect them while they are bearing and nurturing healthy children."*

These physiological differences helped us understand the basic differences between the male and female identity. Where the female is generally more receiving, nurturing and passively receiving, the male is generally more penetrating, acting, and aggressive. For example, Stern explains men tend to attack nature — pushing repeatedly into women to deposit sperm, digging and planting in the earth, cutting down trees and building. In contrast women generally work with nature to passively receive sperm, bear, nourish and care for children.

Males tend to think and process information rationally. In contrast women tend to think and know things intuitively. The most reliable form of truth, the best thinking, is when the male rational and the female intuitive agree. This confirms the Biblical view of creation which describes male and female as in a lifelong interdependent relationship. This is "what the science" — and long experience says.

One of the biggest debates about sexual identity is the nature or nurture question. This is highly relevant to the question of homosexuality. Are people born that way (nature) or is sexual identity formed more by family environment (nurture). In Chapter 5, we quoted Erickson on the research on adolescent play. He noted:

> *"...two distinct psychological trends which are determined primarily biologically and only secondarily by the child's expectation of its social role.*[110]

The biological was the primary criterion in determining sexual identity. The pre-adolescent boys at play chose to build towers and houses — the active, aggressive, creative male. The girls chose to play with dolls — the female passive, nurturing female.

Another psychologist, David Greary, debunks the woke politicized psychology that gender roles are chosen or learned, by reporting research indicating:

> *"...children themselves are the primary impediment to this utopian view. They segregate themselves and create boy and girl cultures. The segregation occurs independently of adult intervention and is one of the most consistently found features of children's behaviour. Children begin to form these same-sex groups*

before they are three years old and do so with increasing frequency during childhood…. Children are not simply imitating sex-typical behaviour or responding to injunctive norms, as they form the same types of segregated cultures in societies in which women and men's social and economic worlds overlap." [111]

The Diagnostic and Statistical of Mental Disorders (Third Edition) was published by the American Psychological Association in 1980, before politicization destroyed its credibility. It defines and classifies homosexuality under "302.0 Sexual Deviations and Disorders." These are described as "Abnormal sexual inclinations…" with homosexuality described as "Exclusive or predominant sexual attraction for persons of the same sex with or without physical relationship." (p. 429) This includes lesbianism. The DSM3 clearly distinguishes this from "Gender-role disorder" (302.6):

"Behaviour occurring in preadolescence of immature psychosexuality which is similar to that shown in the sexual deviations described under transvestitism (302.3) and trans-sexualism in 302.5. Cross-dressing is intermittent, although it may be frequent, and identification with the opposite sex is not yet fixed. The commonest form is feminism in boys."

The difference between pre-adolescent and mature is highly significant and relevant. LGBTQ activists and supporters in schools have done great harm to many children who are simply exploring their sexual identity by prematurely encouraging them to transition medically into a non-birth gender. It is estimated that 80% of these children later regret transitioning and seek psychological, spiritual, and medical help in returning to their birth gender. In Canada this counselling or assistance is now illegal because of politicized and poorly drafted anti-conversion therapy legislation.

Leanne Payne is an internationally known author and counsellor, with probably the most experience in healing prayer ministry for homosexuality. Like John and Paula Sandford, she was a popular healing ministry conference and workshop leader. She authored two books on healing prayer ministry for the sexually confused — *The Crisis in Masculinity* and *Healing the Broken Image*.[112] From her training in psychology she expands on the Sandfords' explanation on how men and women need to be affirmed in their sexual identity by warm, gentle loving fathers (not mothers). She also explains it as calling adolescents into their adult identity.

Payne explains that "The step of self-acceptance comes just after puberty."[113] Puberty or adolescence is a narcistic stage when children are very focused on themselves. They are concerned about their changing bodies and emotions. It is essential that they do not stay in this unhealthy kind of self-focus and self-love and move on to self-acceptance. To love others, you must first love and accept yourself.[114] "Whether we come out of the narcissistic stage depends on the affirmation that comes from the masculine."[115] Payne echoes Sandford in noting that fathers need to clearly affirm both the masculine in men and the feminine in women. Mothers cannot do this.

She explains that the human will is masculine. This is where the human desires of the body meet the divine call for relationship and obedience.[116] Those who chose to enter this relationship, male or female, are made whole persons. They are in touch with their masculine will and free to make unlimited choices in life. "When a man or woman is cut off from the masculine within, his or her capacity to choose wholeness and heaven is in jeopardy." [117] They may need prayer ministry for healing or even deliverance to achieve and freedom of the will in its full power to choose.

Leanne Payne has spent over 20 years leading workshops and teaching pastors, priests, and health professionals how to heal homosexuality. She has a deep knowledge of the truth of homosexuality (including lesbianism) from both a psychological and spiritual perspective. Psychology — the study and care of the psyche or soul — is a very recent attempt at secularizing 2,000+ years of Judeo-Christian spiritual counselling practice and experience in the "cure of souls." Psychology excels at diagnosing psychological conditions and counselling people on how to adapt to reality and more successful behaviour. But it often cannot cure or change people's lives. Prayer ministry has the advantage of millennia of experience in supernatural spiritual warfare that can lead people to real freedom from the inner guilt and shame that often binds them in a pattern of destructive behaviour. The ideal is a combination of psychological counselling and healing prayer ministry. Psychological counselling alone is a little bit like trying to fix a car that runs on gas without using gas.

The bottom line is homosexuality is (or was) considered a mental disorder or sexual deviation from normal male behaviour. This is not a value judgement or a condemnation. It is simply an identifiable psychological difference like abnormal fear of heights or open spaces.

6.4 Recovering the Truth of Male Identity

The crisis in masculinity is a crisis of the truth of male identity and self-worth. This is a real existential problem for our Western culture. Payne echoes Solzhenitsyn's warning in summing up the crisis by writing

"When enough individuals are out of touch with the masculine, a whole society is weakened on every level of existence."[118] She paraphrases Solzhenitsyn saying:

> *"...we in the West are too weak to expose the Communist evil that overcomes and defies intelligent thinking — that we have let ourselves be pushed into a trench dug out for us by communism because of our spiritual weakness.... Consuming more and more, shying away from work, hedonistic, whose family is destroying itself, tempted by drugs, atheistic, paralyzed by terrorism, has lost its spiritual energy, and lost its spiritual health. It cannot survive such as it is."[119]*

We have examined the truth about male identity in the Bible and sciences of physiology, biology, psychology and seen how they all agree on the evidence that sexual identity is binary, interdependent, and designed to continue the divine process of creation. Men are physically, spiritually, and psychologically designed to unite with women and support them in conceiving, protecting, and raising children. This is the lost male and female purpose. Men and women are the most perfect beings in God's creation. They are charged with continuing the stewardship of God's creation. This includes the self-sacrificial love and care of their fellow men and women, particularly those who need help in surviving and thriving in the divine order of creation. This love of God and our neighbour is the spiritual glue that holds the Western foundation of progress together and ensures all are honoured and can prosper. We need to go from judgement and condemnation to acceptance and care.

If we are to survive as a free and thriving democracy (yes, it's an existential problem) we must all work together to challenge and expose the false truth of homosexuality as a normal male — or a normal female.

Some of these men and women have chosen to seek psychological or spiritual counselling and been helped to either adapt to or be healed from their same-sex attraction. This proves the point that sexual dysphoria is an abnormal psychological or spiritual condition that can be healed.

Others have chosen to undergo more drastic transition therapy with counselling, drugs and even surgery to medically adapt to their bodies to their sexual preference. As we have seen above, this is a dangerous path that is out of control. The Tavistock Institute in the U.K. has been closed following a government investigation found children as young as 15 were being moved through chemical and medical gender transition after one interview by one doctor to determine if this would help. A subsequent Government review of sexual transitioning found no robust evidence that sexual transitioning was effective. The only firm evidence was that those who transition experienced harmful outcomes such as depression and thoughts of suicide more frequently than those who did not.[120]

The way to recover the truth of male identity is for the silent majority to engage politically and challenge the false truth of homosexuality as a normal male or female identity wherever they have a voice or vote.

6.4.1: Challenge Churches to Teach Spiritual Truth

The Seven Spiritual truths of the Foundation that our freedom and democracy are built on are defined and explained in Chapter 9.

6.4.2: Challenge Professional Associations to Be Professional about Truth

The credibility of the American Psychiatric Association has been severely compromised by its decision to remove homosexuality or sexual dysphoria from its *Diagnostic and Statistical Manual of Mental Disorders* IV, in response to political opposition and picketing by woke LGBTQ activists. By de-listing sexual dysphoria as a mental disorder; the American Psychiatric Association abandoned its professional responsibility for advancing the truth and knowledge of psychology. As a professional librarian, I stand on the Federation of Canadian Library Association's "Statement on Intellectual Freedom"[121]:

> *"Libraries have a core responsibility to safeguard and facilitate access to constitutionally protected expressions of knowledge, imagination, ideas, and opinion, including those which some individuals and groups consider unconventional, unpopular, or unacceptable. To this end, in accordance with their mandates and professional values and standards, libraries provide, defend, and promote equitable access to the widest possible variety of expressive content and resist calls for censorship and the adoption of systems that deny or restrict access to resources."*

By abandoning its professional responsibility in the face of LGBTQ activist picketing and social media bullying, the American Psychiatric Association provided professional approval of homosexuality as a normal male condition. A tiny mob of the unqualified, the confused and the different now rule over the qualified, the disciplined and the normal. This is the stealth New left Marxist totalitarianism that is now in control of many legal, academic, educational, and medical professional associations — and the clients and students they serve.

This is an internal professional matter so we depend on a silent majority of members of the profession being ashamed, outraged, and electing new board members who will act more professionally and less politically.

6.4.3: Challenge Public Schools, Universities and Colleges to Teach Objective Truth

Our universities and colleges have been politicized and taken over by New Left Marxist, feminist, and LGBTQ activists. As I write, mobs of activists sympathetic to Hamas, a known terrorist organization, guilty of horrific war crimes, are occupying university campuses in Europe and America to protest the Israeli response to their barbaric attack. These protestors are completely delusional in their ignorance of world history and interpretation of the evidence. They are not qualified to participate as informed citizens in a democracy. What is most disgraceful is that the administrators of many of these colleges have refused to request police to remove the trespassers from university property. Many of these demonstrations include blatant hate speech. "From the river to the sea" is a clear call to genocide against the men, women and children who live in Israel. The reason the Palestinians are not free is they and their forefathers have consistently refused to accept the division by the U.K. Government into Palestine and Israel. They have started and lost three wars against Israel.

This ignorance of citizens will be fatal to freedom and democracy in the West. In Chapter 9 I propose defunding public schools, universities and colleges that fail to teach objective truth. They have failed to produce informed citizens who can engage in civil debate and discern truth from opinion.

6.4.4: Challenge Destructive Conversion Therapy Legislation

Most of us have no voice or vote in a profession, but we do have a voice and vote to replace the irresponsible politicians who were intimidated by the woke LGBTQ mob into passing poorly drafted and unbalanced legislation on conversion therapy. The intent of the legislation was good. Forced conversion therapy of any kind is an immoral and ineffective breach of personal freedom. The problem is in the details. The poorly drafted and activist inspired Canadian law on conversion therapy only bans professional counselling and conversion therapy for those considering transition back to birth gender. There are no restrictions on LGBTQ activist or misguided teachers and school counsellors encouraging very vulnerable preadolescent children to explore non-birth genders. This is the root of our sexual identity chaos. As explained above, adolescents are going through a very fragile time as they begin to discover their sexuality. They are confused and need time to mature into their identity. This is where they need a strong, loving, and gentle father to support and call them into adulthood as a man or woman. Children need protection from well-intentioned but misguided and irresponsible teachers, counsellors and activists who encourage them to rush into a non-birth identity. They need a professionally trained psychological counsellor or priest who can remain neutral, answer questions wisely and respect their right to decide when they are mature. The legislation needs to be revised to:

1. Make voluntary conversion therapy and medical assistance illegal before age 18 and

conditional on two hours of neutral professional psychological counselling on the risks
and dangers.

2. Make advocacy for non-binary genders and
    gender conversion illegal in schools with stu-
    dents under 18.

3. Allow professionally trained psychiatrists,
    psychologists and clergy to advertise and
    provide unbiased voluntary counselling and
    prayer ministry for gender exploration and
    conversion (either way) for adults over 18.

The legislative establishment of this truth of conversion therapy will free children from confusing and in-
appropriate advice in schools, give them time to mature and grow into their birth identity — or think about
gender conversion as adults. It will free the 80% of adolescents who were rushed into gender conversion
from the trap of not being able to find and have the psychological, medical, and spiritual counselling and conversion therapy they need as adults.

6.4.5: Challenge Discriminatory Human Rights and Marriage Legislation

Homosexuality has now been protected as a normal
male or female identity by human rights, anti-discrimination, and marriage legislation. This was a well-intentioned but destructive gesture to protect the LGBTQ
community from discrimination in employment. If discrimination based on sexual identity is illegal in employment practices, it is illegal in everything. This is
how the law works and has been manipulated. The
word discrimination has been weaponized and turned
upside down. This is an example of Nazi word manipulation techniques. Discrimination used to be a good

thing. People who could distinguish between a good and poor bottle of wine, clothing, or friends had discriminating taste. This was a compliment and sign of expertise. The evils of racial discrimination changed that. Woke activists have used racial anti-discrimination legislation to both right the wrongs of society and to gain political power ever since. The ultimate obstacle to the sexually confused in having their identity "normalized" or made equal, was Christian marriage. They needed the churches' formal blessing or approval that homosexual couples were not "living in sin" or immoral, that it was the same as or equal to heterosexual couples in the eyes of God.

This is the opposite of what the Bible says. Sadly, because of widespread disunity and failures in Protestant church leadership, many churches now offer the sacrament of holy matrimony to same-sex couples. We have seen the resulting destruction in confused men and women losing their sexual identity and self-worth, dysfunctional marriages, and families unable to raise thriving future citizens.

The social confusion and chaos around human rights and marriage legislation cannot be resolved until there is a psychological, spiritual, political, and legal compromise that differentiates between traditional male-female marriages that have been shown to raise thriving future citizens — and same-sex unions or partnerships that are generally less likely to produce thriving future citizens. It is a case of the minority respecting the primacy of the majority and the majority trying to accommodate the needs of the minority. This is the North American Compromise proposed in Chapter 11 and the best way forward. It will free all men and women to thrive and grow in a loving and honourable relationship that works for them.

7: Diversity, Equity, and Inclusion as False Justice

"Anti-racism can easily devolve from a call to equal justice for all to a demand for power and privilege."
David Frum, *Trumpocalypse: Restoring American Democracy 2020*

Justice is about maintaining order. If there is no order, we have more social chaos (like now) when everyone can say and almost do whatever they like. The authority for maintaining social order evolved historically from the "might is right" of feudal lords, kings, and rulers to the rule of laws, approved and enforced by a government elected by a majority. People in thriving democracies considered themselves under divine authority and law, as approved and maintained by an elected parliament, and administered by the state.

The woke Diversity, Equity, and Inclusion (DEI) movement is the opposite of justice. It is the weaponization of imaginary guilt. While it is true that our ancestors often discriminated against those who were different — not white Christian males, this does not give their ancestors a right of discrimination against white Christian men.

We are back to the lost truth of the divine order and process of creation. The evidence of history (which our schools and universities no longer teach rigorously) is that freedom, participatory democracy, and economic development originated in the predominantly white Christian West. It spread to other countries as Christianity spread. This was not racist, as other races in Asia and Africa have also developed thriving democracies and economies in predominantly Christian countries.

The point is that we are all equal in value and worth as human beings, but we do not all have the same truths, values, and abilities. These truths, values, and abilities, not our race, determine co-operation, competitiveness and success.

The woke Diversity, Equity, and Inclusion movement is deconstructing the truths of divine authority and order. They are replacing these truths with their own false truths and implementing totalitarian rule. This is beyond dangerous in this competitive and hostile world with nuclear arms. Rene Russo warns that:

> *"When an open society becomes an enemy of shared loves, when critical intelligence wages total war against our anchoring convictions, our political consensus becomes anti-human. This is what has happened in the West."*[122]

More specifically, he says:

> *"Modern societies' weak gods of policy expertise, therapeutic delicacy when speaking of sensitive subjects and the rhetoric of diversity and other modes of inclusion have replaced the strong gods of love, solidarity, and truth."*[123]

In this chapter we will expose the truth that the woke activists are doing the opposite of what they say. We will see that woke diversity is really discrimination, inclusion is really exclusion and equity is really inequality. The woke DEI activists learned from the New Left Marxists and environmentalists how successful public sympathy and word manipulation can be as a route to power for the less qualified. DEI activists have created a false problem of injustice which, of course, only they, the unelected elite, can solve. Diversity, inclusion, and equity is not about "doing good." It is a dangerous political power grab by the less qualified, less gifted, and less hard working. They have hijacked the once necessary affirmative action for the disadvantaged into a weapon of advancement for the less gifted, less qualified, and less able to compete. We need to focus and understand how what sounds at first like a "progressive" idea may be dangerous and destructive to truth, freedom, democracy, and economic prosperity.

7.1: DEI Destroys Freedom and Excellence

Diversity, Equity, and Inclusion are the weak gods of our time. They are a woke replacement theology for the Christian values of self-sacrificial love of God and neighbour, the hope of eternal life and fear of divine judgement. They are weak gods because they do not motivate people. They are based on anger, power, and control rather than love, hope and freedom.

They discriminate against the key motivating values and rewards of personal freedom and human excellence. Diversity limits an employer's freedom by requiring them to hire a quota of people by race, disability, religion, gender, or sexual orientation to achieve a mix of employees that matches the mix of different races, religions, gender, and sexual orientations in the wider community.

Inclusion is discriminatory because employers are strongly encouraged to discriminate in favour of less qualified (diverse) applicants over better qualified applicants. This is New Left Marxism by stealth. It is the opposite of the free-market capitalism that our economic prosperity is based on. It is unjust as those who are more qualified may be discriminated against unjustly. It is untrue as the less qualified are treated as the more qualified.

While it is generally a good idea to try to include the disadvantaged if they can do the work, this, like the Christian value of charity, must be voluntary. Instead, organizational "Diversity Officers" now enforce diversity and inclusion. The less qualified are supposed to be given preference — and being human, may take and have taken advantage of this by filing complaints to the Diversity Officer if unsuccessful. This is the weaponization of diversity and inclusion.

The weak god of diversity is given preference over the strong god of truth in deciding who it is best to hire or promote. The employer has lost their freedom of speech and action to decide who is the best qualified candidate.

The morale of staff suffers as opportunities for advancement are missed. Better qualified employees leave to seek advancement in other organizations. There are already consequences. Diversity and inclusion policies are why the quality and standards of work in American businesses are declining. This affects business competitiveness, employment, economic growth.

Diversity, equity, and inclusion policies have also destroyed our schools and universities as places of excellence in learning. Academic test scores in universities, schools, and colleges are declining. For example, to achieve equity in teaching mathematics the proposed California equity policy would:

> *"...effectively close the main pathway to calculus in high school to all students except those who take extra math outside school — which in practice means students from families that can afford enrichment programs (or those going to private schools...)"*[124]*and "we*

reject ideas of natural talents [and the] cult of the genius".

Levine continues:

"And yet the research they cite to justify these claims has been demonstrated to be shallow, misleadingly applied, vigorously disputed or just plain wrong."

This is another example of the false truth of politicized human reason replacing the truth of long human experience. It is the less intelligent and less gifted trying to drag the more intelligent and more competent down to their level. Meanwhile our international enemies are overtaking the West in the math skills on which modern computers and military technology depend.

Equity is discrimination against the values of greater reward for excellence, working harder and better performance. Equity is the socialist goal of equal pay and reward for more (or less) equal performance. Equity is the delusion that government compelled, socialist, Marxist, and communist illusion of equal outcomes for all workers, regardless of performance is just. It is the opposite of the liberal conservative ideal of individual freedom and equal opportunity for all, with outcomes (rewards) based on ability, hard work, and performance. We all know how well the promised workers' paradise of equity worked out in Russia. An elite of less competent communist masters prospered, and the workers sank into poverty, alcoholism, unproductivity, artistic ugliness, and atheistic hopelessness. In practice, success depends on somebody competent being in charge. The real-world objective truth of the survival of the fittest is absolute. If the less fit oversee or the work, the long-term survival of the organization, business or country is at risk. Diversity, Equity, and Inclusion officers are a dangerous step backward into more control, lower staff morale, disorder, less freedom, less creativity, less excellence, and less productivity.

Canada is sadly a model of DEI correctness and the laughingstock of late-night U.S. and U.K TV. In 2023, Canada had a 50% female cabinet including all possible races, religions, sexual orientations and disabilities. The result is daily eye-watering incompetence and embarrassment as hapless cabinet ministers stumble through prepared statements to explain their colossal mismanagement. For example, a decade after other NATO countries, Canada has re-decided to buy the F35 fighter aircraft that the woke Prime Minister had originally dismissed as "not working."

Woke DEI policies are destructive to the values of free market competition, hard work and rewarding excellence. Justice requires rewarding those who contribute more with more, and those who contribute less with less. This is the opposite. It is a New Left Marxist attack on free market capitalism and the Judeo-Christian objective truths our progressive Western culture was built on. It is authoritarian rule by the unqualified and misguided woke mob.

7.2: DEI Policies Deconstruct Democracy

As we have seen, Western social, political, and economic progress is based on a foundation of Judaeo-Christian spiritual truths experienced by many people in many places and times over thousands of years. The biblical truths of self-sacrificial love of God and neighbour hope of eternal spiritual life and fear of divine judgement led to our social order and trust. This foundation of order and trust enabled the Magna Carta, the first real democratic government and the Industrial Revolution to develop in England. Since then, these values have led to more individual freedom and democratic governments in Judeo-Christian countries. In contrast many non-Christian countries without this cultural foundation remain in or have sunk into rule by religious or political despots and poverty. We have recently seen the 20+ years of military support and 200+ billion dollars in aid to Afghanistan fail to develop a functioning democracy.

This is a reminder of a debate in the 1960s — I was there. The US State Department was going to turn Vietnam into a free democracy as a bulwark against the spread of communism. There was a very public dispute between the State Department and the Defence Department who were tasked with restoring order. The military at the time said, and history has taught, "the military doesn't do nation building." Sadly, they were right, but nobody listened. As the poor souls, 50,000+ of whom died for no gain in Vietnam, used to say:

> *"We are the unwilling, led by the incompetent, to do the unnecessary, for the ungrateful."*

Diversity, Equity, and Inclusiveness are the weak gods of spiritually confused atheists. They do not know or respect the truth that the Biblical order prioritized self-sacrificial love of neighbour — charity, care of widows and orphans and protecting the weak from oppression. There are serious eternal consequences for failing in this. The difference is Judeo-Christian self-sacrificial love and charity are voluntary. Each person has the freedom and responsibility to choose what to do. Diversity Officers and policies are the opposite. They take away that opportunity, freedom, and responsibility.

They are trying to replace the wisdom and truth of history with the historically failed ideals of Marxism and socialism.

We have seen the disorder around us as the value of individual freedom in decision making is replaced by the delusional policies of DEI activists. This is the rule of the mob. Specifically, a mob of the different, the confused and the less successful minority. Those with the loudest voices are overruling the democratic wisdom and decisions of the majority. The truth of the right thing to do is replaced by the false truth of political correctness. As we have seen above, the truth of evidence and democratic experience is replaced by the false truth of minority opinion. This is the false justice of the mob. They claim to right a wrong that doesn't exist by discriminating against excellence and hard work. They force the inclusion of those who may not deserve to be included and replace equal pay for equal work with the inequity of equal pay for all of Marxism. This must be challenged.

7.3: Abolish Diversity, Equity, and Inclusion

Diversity, Equity, and Inclusiveness are the opposite of the individual freedom and free market competition on which thriving democracies and capitalism are based. DEI is back door, anti-capitalist New Left Marxism by stealth. It may sound good in theory. The problem is it doesn't work in practice. Instead of freeing people from the exaggerated evils of capitalism and competition, they lose the freedom to compete fairly for more demanding but higher paid work. They are enslaved by a totalitarian elite of DEI officers who can determine who gets the higher paid job.

Diversity, Equity, and Inclusion is a recipe for political and economic disaster. Western free market capitalism has outperformed all other systems. It is based on a solid foundation of the absolute Christian values of honesty (Thou shalt not steal), truth (Thou shalt not bear false witness) co-operation and trust (You shall love your neighbour as yourself) — and the hope of eternal life. These are the truths and values that enabled the first real democracy and Industrial Revolution in England. These are the values that enabled people to trust each other and work together in establishing thriving businesses and international trading companies. The engine was self-interest and competition for profit. Those who worked harder and smarter prospered. The lazy and less gifted did not. It sounds cruel, but this is the reality of human life in this dimension.

The consequence of DEI New Left Marxism by stealth is that instead of having a large pie divided based on contribution to making the pie, we end up with a smaller pie divided evenly. This is not equity and not justice. Survival of the fittest is how nature improves and works. We can't change this. We must adapt or die. It works at the level of individuals, organizations, and nations. This is why diversity, inclusivity, and equity policies in hiring and promoting are destroying our economic competitive advantage over other non-free and non-democratic nations that are trying to destroy us.

The simple truth is that DEI is both unnecessary and destructive. The evidence around us is that there are many gifted people of all races, colours, physical condition, and sexual orientations who have competed for and succeeded in many occupations and professions. Race and colour have nothing to do with gifting and ability. I have worked with highly competent professionals of colour as a teacher in Kenya and priests in Canada and in the Caribbean. Diversity, equity, and inclusion, policies are only destructive - not progressive, and not just.

The right way forward is to challenge diversity, equity, and inclusion policies wherever they are found. This includes churches, schools, colleges, universities, businesses, and government organizations. The staff who promote and enforce these policies are destructive and need to be reassigned or released. In Chapter 10: Recovering Freedom," I propose challenging politicians to defund diversity officers, policies and programs to recover freedom in hiring and promoting staff. This will ensure competitiveness and excellence in schools, universities, governments and business.

8: Death as a False Ending

"For God so loved the world that he gave his one and only Son, that whoever believes in him shall not perish but have eternal life."

John 3.16

Life after death is the elephant in the room of our post-truth culture. It is the hidden issue of our time. If there is life after death, the truth of the Judeo-Christian faith is proven as objective truth. If there is life after death, the false truths of human reason, liberalism, climate emergency, feminism, and LGBTQ, diversity, equity, and inclusion activists are exposed as fraud. If there is no life after death for believers, they are just dead when they die. We would all just live and die without the discipline and order of divine judgement and hope of an eternal spiritual life of joy. The Good news of Christianity is that there is a new spiritual life in heaven that begins with belief in Jesus on earth and continues in heaven when our body dies. This Chapter may save many spiritual lives.

8.1: What Happens When We Die?

The Good News of Christianity is that the Covenant of Jesus created an effective way to forgiveness, freedom from sin guilt and to receive His Holy Spirit. The Holy Spirit guides believers in this life and then carries their soul to Heaven for eternal spiritual life. We know what this spiritual life is like because many people have had visions of heaven or written books following near death experiences. Heaven is consistently described as a place of joy and light that you would not want to come back from. I spoke to a lady in church a few weeks ago who died, went to heaven and "begged them to let her stay." Fortunately for us, she came back to life. You can still see the sparkle and glow of joy in her eyes.

My favourite account is one mentioned earlier, about Howard Storm, who describes a terrifying then joyful experience on YouTube. He was an atheist professor of art at a small US college, married to an atheist and travelling in France. He had food poisoning, terrible stomach pains, and was taken to a hospital for treatment. Unfortunately, neither he nor his wife spoke French, and nobody at the hospital could explain they did not have a doctor on call, and he would have to wait until the next day. His pain got worse, he was suffering terribly and just turned over to die. He describes grey figures coming into the room and taking him away. He thought at first that this was good, the doctor had come. This turned to terror when he realized he could still see his body on the bed. The figures began scratching, biting and doing disgusting things to him. They were demons carrying him to hell. Half delirious, he began mumbling bits of the 23rd Psalm and the Lord's Prayer that he could remember from his childhood. He saw a light coming toward him. It wrapped itself around him and carried him to heaven. It was Jesus. After a long conversation with Jesus, he woke up in his hospital bed. The marriage ended and he became a Christian pastor in California. It is described in the video *Howard Storm's Near Death Experience*:

(youtu.be/Pi3e16JY6UM?si=zSxOdLOgUuoIVsVJ).

The post-Resurrection biblical accounts of Jesus teach us he had a new body which could be both material and immaterial. He could pass through locked doors, eat, and drink with His disciples and appear and disappear in different places. The Resurrection was God's "yes" to the Covenant of Jesus and a teaching that our physical death is a false ending. Our hope of being included in this Covenant and continuing our spiritual life in heaven was the motivating glue of the foundation of truth on which our western freedom and democracy was built. These truths must be recovered, and the foundation restored, or we will continue the descent into social chaos, mass violence and totalitarian rule.

The Christian truth about what happens when we die is the silent fear at the core of our being. We are all temporaries. We know we will all die physically. We all fear death. But is death the end of our human life? The truth of the Bible says "no but" — the "but" is the tricky part. The but warns us that there are **conditions.** These conditions are summarized as "whoever believes in Him." To understand how this works we need to understand the holiness of God, the problem of sin, the Covenant of Jesus and how to become a believer.

8.2: The Holiness of God and Problem of Sin

God desires a covenant relationship of holy love and obedience with us. The problem is God must give us free will to choose to love and obey God — or walk away. Genuine love must be a free choice. God cannot force us to love Him. Sin is a choice to not love and obey God. It is a rebellion against God and His divine rule. It is a failure to fear God, love God and love our neighbour. It keeps us in the position of Adam and Eve, who broke the Covenant and were put out of intimate relationship with God and the Garden of Eden.

Sin separates us from God and means we cannot come into His holy presence in Heaven when we die. One way to think about this is to imagine our soul as a tin can and sin as gasoline poured into the can. When we die our body is buried and our personal spirit carries our soul to heaven to be with God. Heaven is a holy place. God's love is like a holy fire. If our tin can was full of gasoline and we came into God's presence, there would be an explosion. It is not God that is failing to love us. God is not rejecting us. God is protecting us by keeping us away from His holy presence. We have rebelled and excluded ourselves.

To understand how sin works in our daily lives we need to see ourselves the way God sees us. We have all heard the words body, soul, and spirit but few know how they relate to each other. This is critical because sin pollutes our soul, makes us unholy and unable to be in God's holy presence as explained above. Sin also pollutes and weakens our personal spirit so the Holy Spirit may not be able to live inside us and guide us in developing an eternal spiritual life. When we die physically, our polluted and weakened spirit may not be able to carry our soul to heaven. The relationship between our body, soul and personal spirit is hard to understand. I spent a considerable amount of time reading and praying about this and was drawn to the biblical Creation Story in Genesis. In the first creation story God does two things:

1. God forms the man out of clay.

2. God breaths the breath of life into the man.

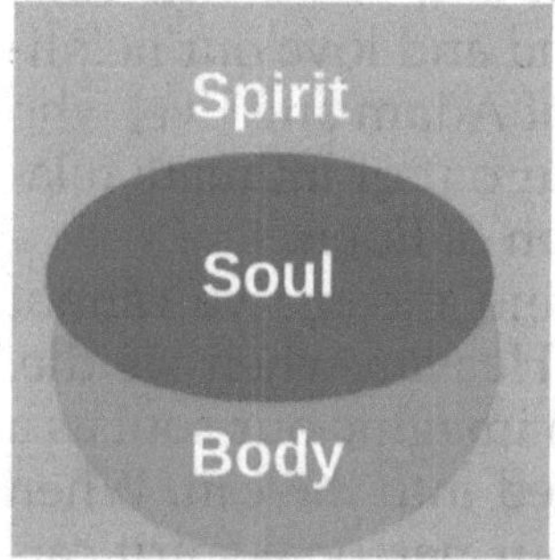

I use a red circle to represent the body and a light blue circle to represent the breath of God —our personal spirit. The overlapping purple circle between the body and personal spirit represents the soul. The point is that our personal spirit is in touch with the divine and is where our intuitive knowledge comes from. This is why women, who are generally more intuitive than men, are more drawn to prayer and church attendance than men.

In the middle is the soul — our mind, will and memory. Our soul is like the meat in the sandwich arbitrating between the holy desires of the personal spirit and the carnal (physical) desires of the body. This is where the spiritual battle takes place The temptations of the body fight for control over the holy desires of the personal spirit. When we regularly give in to temptation and fall into a pattern of sin (e.g. alcoholism); our will (soul) can become polluted and controlled by sin. When our mind/will or soul chooses to listen more to the holy desires of our personal spirit, our personal spirit become dominant. We have chosen to be in a right relationship with God and become a "believer" in Jesus. This right-relationship or righteousness is defined by the covenants God made with Moses and Jesus fulfilled.

8.3: The Covenant of Jesus: Forgiveness of Sin

As explained above a covenant is a formal agreement, like a marriage between the divine and specific individuals. The Bible begins with the covenant of Adam and Eve, which they broke, and were put out of the covenant of eternal life with God. The heart of the Covenant of Jesus is God's promise to forgive the sins of believers who trust in Jesus for forgiveness. God's part in the Covenant was to show self-sacrificial love by giving up His only (biological) Son as a fully divine and fully human and sinless sacrifice for the sins of the world. This was a profound sign of the depth and passion of God's love for the world — the "God so loved the world" part of John 3.16.

Jesus' part was to demonstrate self-sacrificial love for humanity, obey His Father's will, and give up His life for the sins of believers. This was possible because believers were connected spiritually to Jesus through faith. Believers were connected to Jesus in a spiritual relationship. We talk about having a spiritual life "in Christ." Apart from Jesus we do not have a Christian spiritual life. While we do not fully know how things work in the supernatural dimension, we can assume it transcends time. If so, when we demonstrate our belief in Jesus by repenting and asking Jesus for forgiveness, we can imagine Jesus taking that sin back in time to the cross and including it in all the sin He bore on the cross. This sacrifice broke the spiritual power of sin-guilt over mankind — the rod of the oppressor, Satan (Isaiah 9.4).

We die spiritually to our sin when we repent and confess it to an authorized church leader. If it is secret, it has the power of fear, guilt, and shame over us. When it is confessed to a church elder, pastor or priest, that person, as a representative of the Church, has been delegated the authority to pronounce forgiveness in Jesus' name. Some people and churches have trouble with this, but it is biblical. Jesus commissioned His disciples — the leaders of the Church to forgive sins:

> *Again, Jesus said, "Peace be with you! As the Father has sent me, I am sending you." And with that he breathed on them and said, "Receive the Holy Spirit. If you forgive anyone's sins, their sins are forgiven; if you do not forgive them, they are not forgiven."*
>
> *John 20.21–23*

The final step in the forgiveness process is for us to accept this forgiveness. As some people like to hang on to their guilt, those hearing confessions and pronouncing forgiveness in Jesus' name sometimes ask them if they accept this forgiveness from Jesus.

The Covenant of Jesus does not replace the Covenant of Moses but fulfils or completes it through Jesus sacrificial death on the cross. Contrary to what many Christians think, this includes keeping the Ten Commandments. These are the spiritual rules for life and tests of our self-sacrificial love of God and our neighbour (see Exodus 20.1–17).

Keeping the Ten Commandments perfectly is virtually impossible because humans are fallible, weak, deceive themselves and are deceived by Satan. The good news is that divine love covers a multitude of sins so these failures can be forgiven if the intention of our heart is to love God and our neighbour, we repent and ask Jesus for forgiveness. The stumbling block for many people is believing Jesus has the authority to forgive sins and how this works.

The divinity of Jesus is one of the seven spiritual truths of the Bible that is "taken casually" or not believed in our time. If you cannot believe in the divinity of Jesus, the Covenant of Jesus and the forgiveness of sins do not make any sense. This is where many people, including some Christian clergy, fail to become real believers and understand the full benefits of the Covenant of Jesus. The central issue is the divinity of Jesus. If you believe the biblical prophecies are myths and the biblical accounts of the supernatural in Jesus' birth, miracles, Resurrection, and post-Resurrection appearances are exaggerations; you probably believe Jesus was not the divine son of God. Many liberal pastors and clergy believe Jesus was anointed by God but not the biological son of God.

The question is who was the biological father behind Mary's pregnancy? If it was Joseph then Jesus was an ordinary man, he could not die for the sins of the world, there is no life after death and Christianity is only a philosophy of life. If God was the biological father, Jesus could die for the sins of the world, there is life after death and Christianity is a revealed divine truth. As the truth of Christianity and the hope of eternal spiritual life after death is the foundation upon which our freedom, democracy, and economic prosperity rest, we need to get this right.

The Bible is very clear that it was God in the form of the Spirit of God:

> *"The angel answered, "The Holy **Spirit** will come on you, and the power **of the Most High** will overshadow you. So, the holy one to be born will be called the Son **of God**."*

Luke 1.35

Mary and Joseph were not alone. They were being guided and protected by God and His angels all the time. They were warned to flee Herod's planned slaughter of babies in Bethlehem, told when it was safe to come back and heard the prophecy of Anna in the Temple:

> *"Coming up to them at that very moment, she gave thanks to God and spoke about the child to all who were looking forward to the redemption of Jerusalem."*

Luke 2.38

Jesus' ministry was always led by and out of obedience to God. He spent three years walking all over Israel supernaturally healing people from diseases, spiritual blindness, and demonic oppression. Jesus' three-year ministry was a mixture of healing miracles and profound teachings on a life of self-sacrificial love of God and neighbour. This confirmed His authenticity as the expected Saviour. Crowds were drawn to Him, and many became believers.

As there will be some readers who have trouble with healing miracles, let me just say I have been present when a visible spirit of cancer was pulled up and out of a woman's head, seen demons cast out and been praying successfully for healing and deliverance for 30 years. It is real. It is an objective truth — true in many places and times.

The most important part of Jesus' work was to voluntarily show His love and obedience to God's will and His love of mankind by giving up His life for the sins of the whole world. This was His part of the Covenant. Jesus was born to die. Because He was the fully human, fully divine and the sinless "Lamb of God", His death could pay the price for the sins of the whole world. Unlike a lamb or even a human sacrificial death, a divine human sacrificial death could pay for the sins of others. God's part of the Covenant was to forgive the sins of those who believed in Jesus' sacrificial death by asking Him for forgiveness. God's Resurrection of Jesus from death confirmed the Covenant of Jesus,

Jesus' death and Resurrection proved His authenticity as the promised divine Saviour. He showed us the way to forgiveness of sins and eternal spiritual life. Jesus modelled the faith or belief in God that enabled Him to give up His life so others could also be raised to new life. The biblical Resurrection stories include Jesus eating and drinking, going through locked doors and just suddenly appearing. This is the Good News of Christianity.

The biblical and historical evidence of the truth of the divinity of Jesus is consistent from the promise of "another leader like you" to Moses 3,200 years ago to the prophecies of a "servant" in Isaiah 2,600 years ago right up to healing miracles in Jesus' Name in many countries in modern times. The most dramatic and impossible to refute evidence is the growth and spread of Christianity from an outlawed sect of Judaism to the major religion in many countries. Christianity grew because many people continued to experience the Holy Spirit of Jesus and miraculous healings in all places and times. Christianity grew because people could see it was authentic. Not a philosophy but a personal experience of the supernatural — the Risen Jesus.

8.4: Becoming a Believer

Our part in the Covenant of Jesus is to "believe in Jesus." It is not easy to believe in Jesus. Specifically, believing the biblical account of Jesus divinity, supernatural miracles, and Resurrection, and that He could and did give up His life to pay for their sins. The first step is humility in realizing we are sinners and cannot save ourselves by being good.

Most people become believers gradually. They may have had some exposure to Christianity in childhood, gone away from the church as adults and then realized something was missing in their lives. They may feel empty and confused. They may start by talking to friends who seem to have found that "something more" that we are all looking for. They may start by looking for a church community or reading the Bible. Many people are already attending a church but sensing something is missing. They may need to visit other churches to find more relevant teaching or a more spiritually nourishing community. Many people are looking for a good church in our time, as churches go off message on intellectualism or liberal theology.

Often people go through a crisis that drives them to their knees in desperation for answers. In my case it was a divorce. Like many others I had to read the whole Bible and get to know Jesus as a real person. But when I finally cried out, He was there for me and changed my life.

The process of becoming a believer often begins with reading the Bible ourselves. This helps us find out about Jesus. As we go deeper in the Bible we gradually begin to pray. Most people find setting aside a daily time of Bible-reading and prayer is how we go from being a seeker to being a believer. Eventually our prayers are answered. We experience the Holy Spirit and the supernatural in the Bible. Experiences of the Holy Spirit are so compelling we know with certainty the Bible is authentic truth. This is called conversion or being born again or becoming a believer. This was my experience and that of many deeply spiritual people I know.

For most people this can be a lifelong journey to faith. The point is "believing in" is a relationship — not an intellectual affirmation. Nicky Gumbel who developed the Alpha Course explains, becoming a Christian as like falling in love with the woman you married. You just want to be with her all the time, and you know with certainty that this is the one. Just as in marriage the two become one, Christian believers live a spiritual life "in Jesus." We are spiritually connected. Because of this connection we can take our sin guilt to Jesus and ask Him to take it to His cross and give up His life for our sin. Before we can do this, we must repent the sin. This is our personal spiritual death to the sin.

We must also go to the elders of the Church or a priest or pastor and confess the sin. This is critical as our unconfessed sin guilt gives Satan power over us if it is secret. Those who practice "self-confession" can never be free of guilt. Self-confession is a common self-deception.

9: Recovering Objective Truth

"I am the way, the truth and the life."

Jesus Christ *(John 14.16)*

"The truth is always a better idea."

Jordan Peterson, *Rule #8*

"All that is necessary for the triumph of evil is that good men do nothing."

Charles F. Aked

The lesson we have learned is that, as Nietzsche predicted, without a healthy respect for divine truth and authority, things fall apart. Human beings need something higher than other humans to depend on for enforcing order. All thriving democracies have had a Judeo-Christian foundation of divine supernatural truth.

In Chapter *2: Human Reason as False Truth*, we learned that truth based on human reason alone comes down to a power struggle between the opinions of various groups, experts or leaders with the strongest determining what is true. We have lost our way, the way of informed civil debate and majority rule. Civil informed debate has been replaced with word manipulation and bullying. Trump's "Lock her up" defeated the intelligently reasoned arguments of Hillary Clinton. This is where we are in the formerly thriving democracies of the West.

The existential challenge of our time is that we have lost the divine order — the foundation of Judeo-Christian truths. We have lost our fear of divine judgement and hope of eternal spiritual lives. We can lie and cheat without serious consequences. We cannot trust our neighbour. We are back to the totalitarianism of feudalism, rulers and tribalism where might is right.

It is past time for the silent majority to become engaged and challenge and replace the politicians and leaders who have failed them. Specifically, we need to challenge:

1. Church leaders to teach the seven lost supernatural truths of the Judeo-Christian spiritual foundation that our freedom and democracy was built on.

2. Universities, colleges, and schools to teach and affirm objective spiritual, scientific, and historical truth.

3. Professional associations to be professional about truth.

4. Politicians to improve hate speech and disinformation legislation.

9.1: Churches to Teach the Foundation of Truth

> *"Then He opened their minds so they could understand the scriptures."*
>
> *Third appearance of the risen Jesus,*
> *Luke 24.45*

The root cause of the social chaos of our time, as Nietzsche predicted, is the loss of the Judeo-Christian foundation of spiritual truth all thriving democracies depend on. You cannot trust a man who does not fear God. The primary responsibility for recovering the foundation of objective spiritual truth must rest with the Christian church leaders who have a divine mandate to proclaim the basic spiritual truths of the

(Hebrew) Old Testament and (Christian) New Testament of the Bible. The obvious exception is that Jewish rabbis cannot be expected to teach the unique Christian truths of the divinity of Jesus and the forgiveness of sins. They could affirm this as a Christian truth.

This is a call to all churches to co-operate in recovering basic supernatural truths. We all know God will judge us, so beloved, it is in your hands. We are the watchmen on the wall. If we fail to teach the foundation of objective spiritual truths and warn the people, their blood is on our head. If the people ignore our warning their blood is on their own heads (Ezekiel 33.4).

As we have seen the critical foundation of Judeo-Christian supernatural truths, the numinous, was lost in Western culture as the ancient Christian church grew and became intellectualized, politicized, divided and discredited. It lost its authority in maintaining social order. Many Christian church leaders, like their Hebrew forebears who had not experienced the supernatural personally, dropped the ball on supernatural truth. They have not had their minds opened by Jesus. This is why we have so much conflict over doctrine. Some clergy have had their spiritual eyes opened by the Holy Spirit — others have not. The have-nots need to listen to those who have. The Holy Spirit is the Spirit of Truth and the source of all authentic Christian teaching. This is what churches need to recover and proclaim. This is our job #1.

Church leaders have had good reasons for avoiding the supernatural. Those who have experienced the Holy Spirit and dramatic supernatural healing and deliverance ministry have often been spiritually attacked by the demonic and surrounded by conflict and division in churches. But all Christians are called to give up their life of comfort, pick up their cross (the conflict that will kill them physically) and follow Jesus' example of self-sacrificial love. This is a Lenten call to church leaders and teachers to re-think what is being taught in your denomination and provide leadership in teaching and recovering the seven lost spiritual truths:

9.1.1 The Holiness of God

Many Christians are no longer familiar with the Old Testament teachings on the holiness of God and how this relates to sin, salvation, and eternal spiritual life. God is different. God is other. God is not like us. God is the holy, pure, complete, undivided, all-knowing, all-powerful creator of everything. We are unholy, impure, incomplete, divided, and unknowing. The central teaching of the Creation story is that individuals who rebel against God's order, like Adam and Eve, are guilty of sin, become unholy, and cannot be in God's presence. The disobedience of Adam and Eve is called "Original Sin" or "The Fall of Mankind."

This story (a wisdom teaching) explains our spiritual reality of separation from God because we are unholy. The Ten Commandments summarize how to live in an obedient, self-sacrificial and holy love relationship with God and our neighbour.

The Holiness of God is a consistent theme throughout the Bible. For example, Moses is told to take his sandals off because he is standing on holy ground in the presence of God. (Exodus 3.5) At Mt. Sinai the Hebrews are warned, on pain of death; to not come near or let their animals touch the holy mountain or the fire of God's holiness would "break out against them" (Exodus 19.24).

For Christians, the serious consequence is that every time we rebel against God's Commandments (rules) for a holy relationship, we sin. Each sin is like a drop of gasoline in a can. If our soul is polluted by sin when we die; it would be like bringing an open can of gasoline into the presence of the holy fire of God's love.

9.1.2: The Divine Order and Process of Creation

In Chapter 5, we examined the Creation story in Genesis. This story has regularly been dismissed as mythical by extreme liberals or misinterpreted by intellectuals and biblical literalists. It is a wisdom story, revealed by the Holy Spirit and not literal history. Its truth is much deeper than who did what when. Jesus used this teaching technique often to explain the supernatural in natural terms — "there was a man" or "I am the door." The story teaches us that creation is hierarchical, relational, dangerous, competitive and a sign of God's awesome glory and power.

Creation is intentionally hierarchical with God delegating responsibility for stewardship to mankind. Creation is relational. Adam and Eve (we) are intended to be in an obedient love relationship with God and with each other. Love and obedience must include choice, so we each have a free choice, like Adam and Eve, to not love and not obey. But there are dangerous consequences. The relationship is defined in the Bible by divine revelations to the prophets and in the Covenants of Abraham, Moses, and Jesus.

Creation is a continuous process that moves to the ever more complex, successful, and awesome. It started with fish (actually, one cell organisms). The Bible says, "God said let there be fish," etc., which suggests a literal theology of instant one day creation. Darwin's *Origin of the Species* began a storm of debate which sadly blinded many in the Church to the deeper wisdom of the story. Biblical literalists were outraged by the contrary idea of evolution as a natural scientific process that explained, possibly even replaced, the power of God. They missed the point. They dropped the ball. Darwin discovered natural selection, slight differences in offspring — evolution as God's basic biological process in nature. Plants and animals changed and adapted to harsh surroundings to survive — or not, in different environments. This is how creation gets better as more successful changes are more likely to be passed on to the next generation.

Doubters need to look closely at a chicken's lower legs. They will see what looks like fish scales. A fish that could evolve fins into wings and fly short distances, would be more successful in escaping death and more likely to have offspring. Extend the length of a day to a several million years, and the five steps of the divine order and process of creation is consistent with science. Darwin proved that there was an extremely intelligent design based on natural selection, random chance in evolution and survival of the fittest. There was a designer, a process of creation. We call him God.

9.1.3: Male and Female Identity and Relationship

The creation story is also wisdom teaching on the male-female identity and relationship. The relationship is interdependent. The man was alone and needed a "helper" (Genesis 2.18). He could not rule over creation, gather, or grow food, protect himself from dangerous animals, and bear and raise children all at the same time. God created woman out of the body of the man. The work of the man could be more specialized, more focussed, and more successful. He could depend on the woman to be more successful in bearing and raising more thriving children. The man was also motivated to protect the woman and children in a dangerous environment. He could fight, move farther and faster and be more successful in hunting than a man with a child. By working together as interdependent opposites, they could both be more successful — fit, than two men or two women.

9.1.4: How Satan and Spiritual Evil Deceive and Destroy

In Chapter 3, we saw how extreme liberals dismissed clear biblical teachings on Satan and spiritual evil as mythical and pre-scientific superstition. Without specifically saying so, they have subtly re-defined "evil" as human weakness or badness. Modern liberals do not believe in supernatural evil. For "progressives," bad or destructive behaviour is attributed to flawed upbringing and human thinking that must be corrected by psychology and education.

The creation story includes Satan. He deceives Eve into disobeying God's clear instructions not to eat the fruit of the tree of the knowledge of good and evil. This story teaches us how Satan tests our love of God. This is his job description. This is clarified in the Book of Job. God talks to Satan about the faith of Job. Again, it's a wisdom story with a profound spiritual teaching. God **gives Satan permission** to torment Job, to test his faith, but not kill him.

Satan is not mythical and not "equal" to God. Satan is under God's authority. Satan is in a sense doing the "hard testing" work of God's quality control department. This is the "hard testing" we pray about in the Lord's Prayer.

Some churches teach non-biblical heresies such as that once you are baptized or "saved," you cannot fall into sin. The Anglican Baptism liturgy includes a promise that when (not *if*) you fall into sin, you will "repent and return to the Lord." Church leaders who teach that only God can forgive sins, self-forgiveness or that baptized believers cannot sin, are in heresy. They must be challenged to study their Bibles more carefully and read John and Mark Sandford's book *Deliverance and Inner Healing.*[125]

Repeated sin or a pattern of sin can lead to spiritual wounding. Spiritual wounds are like invisible doorways that can allow the demonic to enter our soul and oppress us. Spiritual oppression, if not broken by the confession and absolution of sin, can lead to spiritual bondage or a mental stronghold. These are the spiritually blind and "prisoners" in the mission statement of Jesus. (Luke 4.18) Mental strongholds are the "isms" — irrational addictions to alcoholism, phariseeism, liberalism, fundamentalism, sex, power or a political or religious ideology.[144]

My most important learning about Satan and the demonic was at a workshop on exorcism with Dr. Charles Craft. I learned how dangerous and legalistic things are in the supernatural dimension. There are no exceptions. I have seen a woman visibly healed when she repented believing the lie that she was "no good" at age 5. There are no grey areas, no excuses, and no justifications.

The good news is as Kraft explained, is that like God, Satan must respect human free will. He can tempt but not oppress us without us first giving him a legal reason (i.e., a sin). Many Christian churches need to recover and teach a more complete biblical and practical understanding of Satan and spiritual evil.

9.1.5: The Divinity, Resurrection and Forgiveness of Jesus

"The angel answered, "The Holy Spirit will come on you, and the power of the Most High will overshadow you. So, the holy one to be born will be called, the Son of God."

Luke 1.35

Many Christians and seekers have trouble understanding and believing in the divinity of Jesus. They have not been properly taught the foundational biblical and spiritual truth that the Spirit of God came over Mary and caused her to conceive Jesus. If they cannot understand and believe in this, then they cannot believe in the divinity of Jesus. If Jesus is merely a man like us but anointed by the Holy Spirit after birth, then He logically cannot give His life for the sins of the world. Christianity loses its enormous power to offer forgiveness, and we are all dead in our sins. Christianity becomes a philosophy of loving your neighbour in the hope you can become holy enough to be in God's holy presence when you die. This is a heresy. It is also where many liberal and some evangelical churches are. Churches that fail to teach this foundational truth are in serious error. Their leadership needs to be challenged to repent, ask for forgiveness, and get back to the biblical truth.

Jesus is the one and only divine son of God. The rest of us are adopted brothers and sisters. This is the basis for His authority to die for the sins of the whole world. The sin must be specifically confessed and taken in faith to the Cross of Jesus. Penitents ask Jesus audibly for forgiveness, proving they believe He died for their sin. The sin is prayed back in time to the Cross, paid for and the priest or an authorized elder pronounces the words of absolution in the Name of Jesus. The penitent may also be asked if they accept this forgiveness and be assured the sin is removed from them as far as the east is from the west or with similar words. This spiritual process is the basis of most healing and deliverance ministry as we will see next.

The forgiveness of sin and freeing people from oppression and feelings of guilt is the most important work of the Church. The readings and teaching in sermons should help people identify their sins and give them hope that they can be forgiven, freed from oppression and guilt and grow into a richer spiritual life of joy. The Church has been severely impoverished, made irrelevant and weakened by the loss of this ministry in many liberal churches. Those churches are declining and being replaced by new, more orthodox and Holy Spirit-led churches, that do give people real practical hope and freedom from sin-guilt.

9.1.6: Healing and Deliverance Ministry

> *"The Spirit of the Lord is on me, because he has anointed me to proclaim good news to the poor. He has sent me to proclaim freedom for the prisoners and recovery of sight for the blind, to set the oppressed free, to proclaim the year of the Lord's favour."*
>
> *Luke 4.18–19*

Supernatural forgiveness, healing and deliverance is the distinguishing characteristic of Christianity. Christianity is unique. No other religion can point to the physical evidence of this ministry in many places and times up to the present. The healing and deliverance ministry of Jesus was what drew people to Him. The miracles were evidence of the divine authenticity of Jesus as the long-promised Messiah. Jesus' biblical ministry should be the model for modern Christian ministry.

The heresy of dispensationalism — that the gifts of the Holy Spirit were only dispensed or given for the time of Jesus, has been disproven by historical experience and is not biblical. It was invented by biblically illiterate church leaders who had not experienced the Holy Spirit and were not personally anointed by the Holy Spirit. They badly needed to be challenged.

Healing and deliverance ministry is best explained in the mission statement of Jesus in Luke 4.16–18 above. It begins with proclamation — proclaiming the Good News of God's love, forgiveness, and healing. Jesus was usually speaking of spiritual things. The passage needs to be understood as going beyond the literal and physical, to the invisible battle in the supernatural dimension. For example, proclaiming the Good News leads directly to freedom from the mental prison of spiritual ignorance of God's love, forgiveness and healing and eternal spiritual life. Proclaiming leads to physical and spiritual healing. Jesus did heal the physically sick, lame, and blind. But most of the healing was spiritual. By opening "spiritual eyes," people could see or understand how the testing of Satan and the demonic worked in practice. In Chapter 2, we saw how Satan can blind people to the truth and even imprison them in mental strongholds like alcoholism. They both hear, but do not hear the truth — this is psychological self-deception working with demonic temptation and oppression. Ultimately Jesus came to proclaim the Good News to "set the oppressed free." This includes the economically, politically, militarily and the spiritually oppressed.

The people you see in thriving, Holy Spirit-anointed churches radiate a love, joy and peace that is visible. This is what many people are now going from church to church seeking. This is the supernatural spiritual truth that has been lost in many churches and needs to be recovered and taught in all Christian churches.

9.1.7: The Holy Spirit as the Continuing Presence of Jesus

> *"When the Advocate comes, whom I will send to you from the Father—the Spirit of truth who goes out from the Father—he will testify about me.*
>
> *John 15.26*

Jesus established His divine authenticity and authority by healing the physically sick, freeing the spiritually oppressed and giving new and wonderful teachings that people knew intuitively were the truth. Jesus promised to send the Holy Spirit to all believers at the end of His earthly ministry (John 15.26 above). The theology of the Nicene Creed and the Trinity explain the relationship of love and unity of God, Jesus, and the Holy Spirit. In simple terms Jesus is God, the Holy Spirit is God, and the Holy Spirit is Jesus with us.

Clergy and church leaders who have not experienced the Holy Spirit cannot fully understand or believe in Holy Spirit. This is an "incomplete faith" as the Roman Catholic Church so graciously would say. Unbelief in the reality of the Holy Spirit is contrary to all the Christian creeds — and fatally dangerous to having an authentic spiritual life.

Jesus promised to pour out the Holy Spirit on all believers. The word "believers" is important. The Holy Spirit cannot live on a spiritual garbage dump. The assumption is that by the time someone becomes a believer, they have begun the self-examination, repentance, confession, and absolution process, to clean out their spiritual garbage.

The Holy Spirit is under the same prime directive as God and Jesus. He cannot come uninvited. Unlike Satan who always tries to control the divine order of love between God and man demands free will. The Holy Spirit will not come uninvited.

The Holy Spirit is the Spirit of Truth, helping us understand the teachings of Jesus. As the continuing presence of Jesus in the world, the Holy Spirit comes to believers with an amazing outpouring of spiritual gifts — love, joy, peace, patience, kindness, gentleness, and healing. These practical gifts help us begin to experience our personal ministry and eternal life of joy in this dimension.

We must be very careful about hearing words of knowledge and being guided by the Holy Spirit. Satan can counterfeit these gifts and has led many astray. This is why we need regular bible study, prayer, and a Holy Spirit-led church community to teach us and confirm, question, or challenge our experiences of the Holy Spirit.

9.2 Defund Failed Universities and Schools

In Chapters 3 to 8 we have seen how freed from the fear and order of divine judgement, political activists were able to redefine truth as minority opinion. Recovering this spiritual foundation of truths will make citizens less likely to lie and deceive others in science and all truth. Over the last 30 years this minority opinion as truth has polluted and degraded all the academic disciplines as less competent but politically correct teachers were hired and rose to power in the education system. There has been a massive failure in the teaching of the objective truths of the Bible, science, history, language (essay writing and debating) and the social sciences. This has been a massive professional failure in the governance of schools, colleges, and universities.

The public education system including schools, colleges and universities has failed to produce informed citizens who can distinguish between truth and opinion, participate in civil debate, and vote intelligently in democratic elections. Freedom and democracy cannot and will not survive if this generation is not engaged and challenged to become better informed and able to participate in civil debate.

It is an existential threat to freedom and democracy to continue funding these schools, colleges, and universities. There is a crisis in public education. Politicians must be challenged to defund universities, colleges, and school boards until they dismiss the administrators and teachers who have politicized truth and are not adding value to public education and the state. There is no serious body of knowledge and value in the new woke courses and pseudo disciplines such as gender studies, women's studies, aboriginal studies etc. They are simply make-work projects and minority propaganda. Jordan Peterson suggests 90% of university administrators and half of the students and faculty should go.[126]

This does not mean that everyone must become a Christian believer. It does mean that the objective spiritual teachings of the Bible — and other great religions, must be taught in public schools. The objective truths of the foundation must be known and respected as part of objective human history. These are the objective truths that all schools, universities and colleges should have a civic and professional obligation to teach and affirm. The failure of those who sit on public school, university and college boards must be challenged. They must recover the teaching of objective truth in curriculums or face defunding. Political leaders should be challenged to enforce this responsibility in government funded educational institutions. Those who argue it is offensive to non-Christians are simply deluded and trying to avoid dealing with their own lack of knowledge, faith, or reality.

9.3 Challenge Professionals Who Failed Us

In Chapter 6, we saw how sexually confused woke LGBTQ activists picketed and interrupted an annual meeting of the American Psychiatric Association until they promised to remove "sexual dysphoria" (confusion) from their official list of psychological disorders. The woke LGBTQ activists and their well-meaning but dangerously naïve supporters, have used social media very effectively to lobby and bully other professional licensing bodies in psychology, education, and law to uphold their false truths about sexual identity. In Canada, the Ontario Psychological Association published new politicized guidelines for practice that are the opposite of the professionally observed truth and professional research on masculinity. This reversal of professional truth is the direct cause of the emotional pain and social chaos of men and women who don't know who or what they are. This has resulted in dysfunctional relationships, and families unable to nurture thriving future citizens. This is costing governments millions of dollars in welfare, underemployment, and criminal justice costs. These costs are born by the silent majority that the educators and professional associations are supposed to serve and help. The unprofessional politicians on professional governing bodies need to be challenged and replaced with real professionals who will protect the truths of the profession.

As a professionally trained librarian with a master's degree in library and information science, I find this an outrageous betrayal of professional responsibility for developing and maintaining the objective truth of an important body of knowledge. The library profession has a "Statement on Intellectual Freedom" that specifically demands the right to collect and make available material on subject matter that may offend some readers. The unprofessional politicization of truth has now spread to other professions that are supposed to be guardians of objective truth:

- Law Societies have become politicalized and failed to enforce neutrality and protect legal truth by requiring members to affirm and defend the false truths of extreme feminist and LGBTQ activists and the legislation that protects them.
- Medical Associations have become politicalized and failed to enforce the "do no harm" of the profession on doctors who facilitate irreversible sex changes on children before they have had time to mature, adapt to their biological sexual identity and give informed consent.

I went to the University of Alberta in the 60s. The motto was and still is *Quaecumque vera* — "whatsoever things are true" (Philippians 4.8). This should be the standard for all professionals, regardless of their political opinions and personal experiences. The members of these professions need to challenge their leadership and board members to act professionally or be replaced. Provincial governments should be challenged to suspend the licensing of professional associations that fail to protect objective truth.

9.4 De-Politicize Hate Speech Legislation

"Speech that is intended to insult, offend, or intimidate a person because of some trait (such as race, color, national origin, religion, gender, sexual orientation, gender identity, or disability)[127]*"*

Woke activists have politicized hate speech legislation to protect their false truths of sexual identity, economics and history from civil debate and criticism. They have established a cultural norm of political correctness, where offending someone is unacceptable. Being offended is in the eye of the beholder, subjective and a natural consequence of civil debate. Political correctness enforces woke totalitarianism. This is an existential problem for truth, freedom of speech and democracy. Objective truth, what has been seen to be true and has not been disproven. It is discerned through informed civil debate of all the evidence. Civil debate is going to offend those whose ideas are criticized or rejected. This is considerably less harmful than the alternative of settling debates by physical violence.

Governments in Canada the U.K and Australia are struggling to agree on a practical, enforceable and non-political definition of hate speech. In Canada hate speech is defined in the Criminal Code, sections 318 and 319:

- *318 (1) Every person who advocates or promotes genocide ....*
- *(b) deliberately inflicting on the group conditions of life calculated to bring about its physical destruction.*
- *319 (1) ... communicating statements in any public place, incites hatred against any identifiable group where such incitement is likely to lead to a breach of the peace...*
- *(2) ... wilfully promotes hatred against any identifiable group...*
- *(Marginal note: Defences — subsection (2.1)*
- *No person shall be convicted of an offence under subsection (2.1) if they*
- *(a) establish that the statements communicated were true.*

- *(b) if, in good faith, they expressed or attempted to establish by an argument an opinion on a religious subject or an opinion based on a belief in a religious text.*
- *(c) if the statements were relevant to any subject of public interest, the discussion of which was for the public benefit, and if on reasonable grounds they believed them to be true; or*
- *(d) if, in good faith, they intended to point out, for the purpose of removal, matters producing or tending to produce feelings of antisemitism toward Jews.*[128]

This Canadian legislation is deeply politicized and contradictory. Many Islamic extremists "sincerely believe" god hates the Jews. It politically protects religious belief or opinion – the most common source of hate speech. This directly contradicts the antisemitic clause and explains why police do not bother to arrest and charge the Islamic spiritual and religious leaders teaching hate. Religious belief and practice is not above the law of the land.

The Canadian legislation is also politically compromised as prosecution depends on the approval of the Attorney General. The helpful part is that truth is protected, and breeches of the peace are given as a semi-concrete measure of harm. This is compromised by the vagueness of "likely" and breaches of the peace. A revised version of this Canadian legislation is currently under review and stalled in Committee.

The U.K is also involved in a political division over its attempt to define hate speech. An in unpassed revision of its 1986 *Public Order Act* defines hate speech as:

- *"...uses towards another person threatening, abusive or insulting words or behaviour, or*

- *distributes or displays to another person any writing, sign or other visible representation which is threatening, abusive or insulting,*
- *with intent to cause that person to believe that immediate unlawful violence will be used against him or another by any person, or to provoke the immediate use of unlawful violence by that person or another, or whereby that person is likely to believe that such violence will be used or it is likely that such violence will be provoked."[129]*
- *The Malicious Communications Act 1988 in the United Kingdom makes it illegal to send threatening, abusive, or offensive messages to others..."[130]*

The U.K. definitions of hate speech are hopelessly vague, impossible to enforce and have confused both police and public. "Insult" and "offensive" are in the eye of the beholder and have been used by activists to protect hate speech, threaten and bully critics, deny freedom of speech and limit civil debate.

In the Revised Statutes of Australia (2024), Section 80 defines hate speech as:

- *80.2A Advocating force or violence against groups*
- *80.2B Advocating force or violence against members of groups or close associates*
- *80.2BA Threatening force or violence against groups*
- *80.2BB Threatening force or violence against members of groups or close associates*
- *80.2BC Advocating damage to or destruction of real property or motor vehicle*
- *80.2BD Threatening damage to or destruction of real property or motor vehicle*
- *80.2BE Advocating force or violence through causing damage to property*

- *80.2C Advocating terrorism*
- *80.2D Advocating genocide*
- *80.2DA Aggravated offence for religious officials or other spiritual leaders etc.*

This definition is a step in the right direction as it goes beyond threats, bullying and intimidation to use advocating or clear threats of violence and acts of violence as a more concrete measure of intimidation and harm. Creating an "aggregated offence" for religious and spiritual leaders is also an important step forward. Islamic extremists have been using freedom of religion as a defence to preach hate with impunity for decades. It is past time to stop treating whatever someone says is their religion as above criticism.

Australia's proposed 2026 *Combatting Antisemitism, Hate and Extremism* bill has been withdrawn as too controversial. It also made the critical proposal to give The Home Affairs Minister broader powers to deny or revoke visas for individuals engaged in hateful, vilifying, or extremist conduct. Sadly, naïve Western liberal democracies have chosen helping foreign students and refugees over the peace order and good government of the nation.

The question is how to define the harm, the damage and the offence of hate speech. The harm needs to be defined in terms that are not vague and open to interpretation. We need to define hate speech in the same way we define other crimes. It needs to be evidence-based not philosophically based. Murder has the evidence of a body. Theft has the evidence of something missing. The evidence of hate speech is the harm that has been seen to be done as result of the speech:

1. Evidence of physical violence against people associated with a group – terrorist attacks, assault or mob violence.

2. Evidence of property damage – homes, places of worship, businesses and cars.
3. Evidence of financial damage – debanking.
4. Evidence of damage to freedom of speech, deplatforming and the process of civil debate on which democracy depends.

Hate speech is intimidation by advocating, advancing or threatening harm to anyone associated with an identifiable group that has been seen to lead to physical violence, property damage, financial loss or to loss of freedom of speech. Hate speech damages civil debate and the democratic process. It is an existential threat to the survival of democracy.

Enforcing hate speech legislation is not working. It cannot work without a clear definition of intimidation and the harm that has been seen to been done. Police need to be freed from the politics of the government and focus on the small number of situations where major harm has been seen to have been done because of specific hate speech by an author, public speaker teacher, blogger or social media post.

We must hold the religious leaders, teachers and public speakers who are the main spreaders of hate speech accountable. We have seen how naïve liberal governments have failed us by allowing the spread of hate speech by religious extremists claiming freedom of religion. This is intolerable. Freedom of religion is a right to practice a religion – within the laws of the country. There should be no place in a Western democracy for hate speech. Non-citizens, students, immigrants and refugees who cannot leave their religious and political hatred behind should be denied citizenship, without appeal and sent home.

Citizens who are spiritual or religious leaders should be charged with an aggrieved hate speech violation and sentenced to prison for many years on the Australian model.

Hate speech is policed by "community standards" on many social media platforms. This is an enormous task as there are an estimated 500 million posts per day on X/Twitter. The problem is that social media platforms 'community standards' are not clear, and the process is neither transparent or fair. The community standards generally use the standard of "offending" — code for not offending the woke activists. The problem as I said is that offence is in the eye of the beholder. The civil debate on which freedom and democracy depend, is going to offend those whose ideas are criticized or rejected in the debate. Political correctness is woke censorship. Minority woke activists have been able to impose their truths on the majority through this social media bullying.

The Community Standards process is also not transparent. A computer filter detects a red word, or an unknown person makes an unknown complaint to a computer and your post is removed. You get a chance to appeal and sometimes are lucky — sometimes not. Social media platforms should be required to implement a fairer and more transparent procedure. For example:

1. Define hate speech and specifically what subjects are not for discussion.

2. Tell the author exactly what was objected to, including the wording of the complaint.

3. Allow an appeal to a human adjudicator where there are serious and equal consequences for both author and complainant.

This might reduce the number of complaints to a manageable level and ensure the complainant is not using the complaint process just to silence the author.

Hate speech can also be posted on fake accounts where the author can hide behind a false identity. Facebook and others are beginning to offer verified identities to give users some assurance that there is a real person or entity behind the account. Social media platforms must be required to do more to be able to identify the people behind the accounts and help police investigate instances of serious hate speech harm.. This is an important step in the right direction to policing internet content.

Police intervention and criminal prosecution comes later when the harm can be clearly seem and linked to an author, publisher, broadcaster, or public speaker

9.5 Criminalize Spreading Harmful Disinformation

> **"Disinformation:** *false information deliberately and often covertly spread (as by the planting of rumors) in order to influence public opinion or obscure the truth"*[131]

Disinformation is not true and intentionally not true. It is intended to deceive or confuse the public and harm the civil debate process that democracies depend on. This makes spreading harmful disinformation an existential threat to a healthy democracy. A recent poll reported on PBS News (December 31, 2024) estimated 70% of Americans consider disinformation an existential issue. Many people have given up on participating in civil debate for fear of conflict and social media bullying by activists. Mass citizen participation in healthy and informed civil debate is essential to democracy.

Tragically in the West we do not even have an informed citizenry. I have explained above how churches, schools, universities and professional associations have been politicized and failed in their responsibility to produce informed citizens. Human rights and hate speech legislation has been weaponized by minority radicals to impose their harmful disinformation on climate change, sexual identity, history and economics on the majority. The consequence is that 86% of 15-year-olds in the U.S. could not distinguish between opinion and truth on a nation-wide study.132

The way forward is to criminalize spreading disinformation that has been seen to cause material harm to citizens or to the state by harming freedom of speech and or civil debate. Examples would include:

- Religious leaders have historically been seen to spread harmful disinformation against Jews that led to genocide, mob violence and property damage.

- The New Left Marxist, Environmentalist disinformation on climate change wasted billions of dollars on subsidies and harmed economic development,

- Governments, medical officials and vaccine suppliers spread harmful disinformation of vaccine effectiveness during Covid 19 that cost millions of lives.

- Diversity, Equity and Inclusion activists spread harmful disinformation on history and race that has seriously damaged the quality and competitiveness of our businesses, schools and universities.

- China has been seen to produce and spread harmful disinformation about political parties and candidates that affected election results

It is not possible for governments to police the millions of social media posts generated hourly. Governments can require social media platforms to have a clear, fair and equitable procedure for reviewing complaints as described above. Current practice is politically motivated to protect criticism of woke false truths of sexual identity, economics and history. This is woke totalitarianism. The standard for harmful disinformation needs to be "seen to lead to material harm to individuals, the state or freedom of speech and civil debate".

Possible breeches can be detected in social media through keywords and complaints. It is the process of adjudication that needs to be improved. Woke activists can easily complain and shut down anyone who challenges their view. Authors can appeal. I was successful but many are not. The problem is the author does not see the complaint and is at a disadvantage in defending the post. This process needs to be refined to filter out frivolous complaints and punish authors and sites that spread harmful disinformation or try to silence others and harm civil debate The ideal would be to refine the complaint process to and make adjudication by a real person possible.

Police intervention comes later when the harm can be clearly seem and linked to an author, publisher, broadcaster, or public speaker. By requiring social media to have clear, fair and enforceable standards, and criminally prosecuting a small number of the major offenders who have been seen to spread harmful disinformation we can recover truth, freedom and the informed civil debate democracy depends on.

9.6: Revise Immigration, Citizenship and Refugee Policies

Naïve and irresponsible politicians have devalued the spiritual truths that underpin all thriving free democracies by welcoming refugees, students and immigrants from failed states with opposing spiritual truths. We have recently seen the fruit of this in massive demonstrations led by Islamic activists against Israel, Jewish schools and places of worship. Many of these activists are on student visas, immigrants or refugees seeking citizenship. They have come from failed states, looking for a better life. But they have brought their religious beliefs with them and not been required to respect our Judeo-Christian truths and values as a condition of entry and citizenship. The result is they are weakening the foundation of spiritual truths all thriving democracies depend on.

Canada has had a decade of a Prime Minister who openly declared we did not have any national identity or national values. This has seriously weakened the country, freedom and democracy.

Freedom and democracy are worth fighting for. The silent majority needs to engage and be more responsible in voting for politicians at all levels of government who will define, uphold and protect the spiritual foundation of truth our freedom and democracy depend on.

10: Recovering Freedom

Freedom of speech and political action has only developed and thrived in countries with a solid social foundation of Judaeo-Christian spiritual truths. Freedom depends on a culture where most people know and respect the need for self-sacrificial love of neighbour, fear God's judgement and the hope of an eternal spiritual life. These beliefs compel them to trust and co-operate with others and respect their needs. They can forgive, accept the will of the majority, and generally trust in the good intentions of the other.

Woke activism is the opposite. Woke activism is not motivated by these beliefs to trust, co-operate with others or respect their needs. Woke activists generally do not love their neighbour, fear God's judgement, or have the hope of eternal spiritual life. Their lives are very limited, unhappy, and motivated by anger against those who they feel criticize or oppose them. It's called "cancel culture." This is "progressivism" as the opposite of progress. Wokeism is a regressive totalitarian minority power grab that is limiting our freedom to criticize or propose alternative viewpoints. This is the opposite of the free, informed civil debate and clash of opinions decided by majority vote that democracy depends on.

The discriminatory false truths of the woke minorities have now been embedded in discriminatory Human Rights, Anti-discrimination, Marriage, and Conversion Therapy legislation. These false truths are now legally protected and enforced by quasi-judicial Human Rights Tribunals and the criminal justice system. They are also broadened and enforced through destructive diversity, equity and inclusion policies in churches, universities, schools, government, professional associations, and businesses. These once justified, but now revised and destructive laws, regulations and policies must be challenged and revised now, before we completely lose our freedom of speech and action.

10.1 Cancel Diversity, Inclusion and Equity

In *Diversity, Inclusion and Equity as False Truth*, we exposed the lie that it is somehow "just" to implement hiring and promotion policies that "affirm" (favour) identifiable minorities, to right the discrimination they or their ancestors may or may not have suffered. In practice this means to discriminate against white Christian men, who may be equally or better qualified and better suited to a particular position. This is basically a woke power grab by the different, the aggressive, the less qualified and the less successful. DEI policies are false justice based on a crime supposedly committed by someone else, designed to win sympathy, gain advantage, and make these minorities "more equal." These affirmative action programs, while once justified, are no longer necessary and are socially and economically destructive. The old affirmative action policies have now been weaponized by woke activists to implement stealth New Left Marxism. They are the opposite of the successful biblical, historical, and capitalist "survival of the fittest" model on which our progressive Western freedom, democracy and economic progress is based.

Diversity and inclusion policies have undermined the authority and freedom of employers and managers to hire and promote based on merit, qualifications, and potential contribution.

Equity is the Marxist delusion of equal pay for unequal contribution. The result has been a decline in morale, productivity and excellence in schools, universities, government, and business. This is beyond dangerous and an existential challenge in our competitive, hostile, and nuclear-armed world.

Recovering our freedom of speech and action in hiring and promotion will be a serious political struggle for power between the silent majority and the various woke minorities. It must begin with many ordinary citizens becoming engaged and influencing the political actors where they live, work and vote. Diversity officers, policies and the programs that support them must be defunded by local, regional and national political bodies to recover freedom in hiring, promotion and recover competitiveness and excellence.

Political actors have no power of their own. They sit on school boards, university boards, town councils, boards of directors and boards of universities, businesses, professional associations and on government committees. Like members of parliament and provincial legislators, they all must run for re-election and fear not being re-elected. They need to be challenged with the truth about diversity, inclusion and equity policies exposed here and challenged to eliminate these economically and socially destructive policies or be replaced. Your local political actors and commentators need to know there is a groundswell of opposition to what the deluded woke activists have done to our once thriving schools, universities, governments, businesses, and culture. Everyone can "like" relevant blogs or write a comment. Decision makers and political actors need a big shake-up, like a defeat in re-election, to notice that many people (their employers) are angry with them for caving in to socially destructive woke minority political bullying. We need a major upgrade and change of political and organizational leadership. The good news is this has already started. — but much more needs to be done.

10.2 Revise Conversion Therapy Legislation

In Chapter 6, we exposed the travesty of conversion therapy legislation that fails to protect adolescents from LGBTQ activists and sympathizers, facilitates changes to a non-birth identity and then criminalizes conversion back to birth identity. This frees activists, teachers, and unqualified school counsellors to encourage immature students to explore sexual identities and transition away from birth identity.

Experience has shown that more than half of those who transition as adolescents decide later as adults to transition back to birth identity. Current Canadian legislation does not provide safeguards for adolescents transitioning away from birth identity but criminalizes professional counselling and transition therapy back to birth gender. This protects the LGBTQ community from facing the truth that psychological counselling and professional healing prayer ministry have proven effective in restoring men and women to healthy birth identity gender relationships.

Current legislation is a breach of personal freedom that is causing great harm to the majority and only benefiting the minority. The silent majority need to support and elect politicians who will challenge and revise this legislation to restore personal freedom and the interests of the majority.

10.3 Abolish Canadian Human Rights Tribunals

These tribunals operate outside the Canadian justice system and outside the usual rules of legal fairness. The people on these tribunals are not necessarily lawyers and may often be feminist or LGBTQ activists or sympathizers. It is not a neutral court. While the expenses of the person making the complaint are covered by the tribunal, the accused must pay their own expenses. The accused is motivated to settle out of court to avoid a significant fine and legal expenses. The result is intimidation and a loss of justice and free speech. The threat of a complaint may be sufficient to force an employer to hire a less qualified applicant. This has happened regularly in our schools, universities, and professions. It has led to a serious measurable decline in education standards and the quality of professional work as we have seen above. American scores on testing standards in 2024 were the lowest in any year on record.

It is past time for the silent majority to become engaged and support political candidates who will abolish human rights tribunals and move the protection of human rights back to the regular justice system.

11: Recovering a Democratic Compromise

Democracy is in decline around the world and dictatorships are growing stronger. The Swiss philosopher and theologian Francis Schaeffer warned, "No totalitarian authority nor authoritarian state can tolerate those who have an absolute by which to judge that state and its actions." [133] Woke activists are the different, the wounded, the less competent and the spiritually and sexually confused. This small aggressive minority has won a political power struggle with the normal, the healthy, the competent, and the spiritually and sexually secure (but silent) majority. This is the opposite of democracy. Democracy was built on a foundation of shared Judeo-Christian truth and order, informed citizens, the clash of opinion in civil debate and majority rule.

David Frum's "North American Compromise" explains what has been lost and needs to be rebuilt.[134] The democratic ideal of the North American Compromise is that the majority rules but tries to accommodate the needs of the minority, while the minority accepts and tries to adapt to the will of the majority. This model works best when both the minority and the majority are aware they are under the sovereignty of God (In God we trust) and will face divine judgement when they die. This is the social model that North American freedom, democracy and prosperity was built on. The countries that have adopted this model have the most thriving democracies and economies.

This North American Compromise worked successfully until recently. As the Christian Church lost its spiritual truths and authority, the woke activist minority launched aggressive media and social action campaigns that challenged the Western foundation of objective spiritual truth and social order and upended the North American Compromise. The minority woke mob has turned this compromise upside down to impose their minority will on the majority. They do not accept the rule of the majority. They have now imposed their false truths, by law in some cases, on the sleeping majority. The silent majority needs to become informed and challenge politicians to revise the destructive legislation that gives the woke minority control over the majority and recover the North American Compromise.

11.1 Find a Compromise on Marriage

In Chapter 5, we exposed the social chaos, damage and economic cost of the sexual identity crisis facing many men and women. The famous Jukes family study over 5 generations in the US revealed the difference between one unmarried atheist couple, the Jukes (not the real name), and Christian the Edwards family. In the Jukes family:

> *"366 were paupers, while 171 were criminals; and 10 lives have been sacrificed by murder. In schoolwork 62 did well, 288 did fairly, while 458 were retarded two or more years. It is known that 166 never attended school; the school data for the rest of the family were unobtainable. There were 282 intemperate (alcoholics) and 277 harlots. The total cost to the State has been estimated at $2,093,685 (1915)."*[135]

The social and economic cost to the state of one atheist unmarried couple was enormous. We also examined

David Frum's evidence showing significant underachievement in children of families without long-term male-female parenting.

We need to recover the special definition of male–female marriage in a compromise where same-sex relationships be described as partnership or unions but not marriages. This is in keeping with the North American Compromise whereby the majority rules and tries to accommodate the minority; and the minority accepts the rule of the majority and tries to adapt to it.

11.2 Find a Compromise on Abortion

Abortion is an explosive issue for many people. In Chapter 5, we examined abortion as the most extreme example of the devaluation of women, and specifically the intuitive nurturing female.

While the monetary cost of abortions may be covered by health insurance, the emotional and spiritual consequences are not. Stein observed that women do not grieve after the abortion. They are wired to the rhythm of nature and grieve later when the baby would have been born. This is biology speaking authentic truth to our politicized truth. There are also spiritual consequences including lifelong feelings of guilt which psychology cannot relieve. The good news is the Church can free people from this — the bad news is that most women would not think of going to a Church.

The abortion debate has sadly descended into meaningless clichés, word manipulation, sound bites and demonization of the other side. The loudest and most extreme voices overrule the quiet voices of compromise and reason. "Pro-life" for example is a meaningless statement that dismisses opponents are "pro-death." "Pro-choice" is also meaningless as it implies the opponent is against all freedoms.

The most popular feminist slogan is "our bodies ourselves." This is an example of very effective but very destructive New Left Marxist word manipulation. The statement is both meaningless and the opposite of truth. It is untrue because abortion involves three bodies. There is the man who contributed the sperm, the woman who contributed the egg and the fetus which has a separate but temporarily attached living body. The woman does have the right to decide what to do with her body. She could have used birth control, asked the man to use birth control, abstained from sexual relations or given the child up for adoption. These are all her choices, and no reasonable person would dispute this.

The issue is really when life begins. There are four strongly held opinions on this — at conception, when there is a separate heartbeat, when the fetus could survive on its own, and at birth. Abortion after each of these points is considered murder — intentional killing of a human being against their will.

Most countries have already found a compromise, where abortion would always be an option for those with a serious medical, psychological, or moral need; and discouraged for those who only find pregnancy and child rearing a temporary inconvenience.

Irresponsible politicians who use abortion as a wedge issue to divide people and win elections need to be replaced with more responsible candidates who will find a fair compromise.

I propose going back to what David Frum calls the North American compromise: "...where the majority tolerates and accommodates the minority; and the minority in turn adapts to and accepts the predominance of the majority."[136] The key will be to challenge politicians to affirm the nurturing female identity by revising marriage, abortion and human rights legislation that devalues female child nurture and male-female marriages. We need to recover the divine order of creation and male-female relationships with a compromise that frees and values the natural gifts of all women.

Sadly, opportunistic politicians have often ignored the wider interest of the state. It is in the long-term interest of the state that the best and the brightest bear and raise ever more successful future citizens. Irresponsible politicians who use abortion as a wedge issue to divide people and win elections need to be replaced with more responsible candidates who will find a fair compromise

11.3 Find a Compromise on Conversion Therapy

We also examined the psychological and medical damage around new Conversion Therapy legislation in Canada which is replicated in other countries. This legislation is the crowning achievement of the LGBTQ activists' victory over truth and freedom of speech and action. As explained in Chapter 6, homosexuality is a spiritual and psychological disorder — despite what the psychological profession has shamefully been bullied into saying. We have seen that homosexuality is not genetic and often related to poor parental modelling and sexual abuse. We know it is a disorder because we know some homosexual men and women have been voluntarily restored to a normal attraction and marriage to an opposite sex partner through psychological counselling and prayer ministry. I have talked to them and explained above how men and women have been restored to their biological identity through a combination of professional psychological counselling and anointed Christian healing and deliverance ministry.

The problem with conversion therapy is that a very small number of unchristian and misguided evangelical pastors "helped" distraught parents by forcibly putting their children through their misguided idea of prayer ministry. They bullied, shamed, and brainwashed a few children into resuming their birth identity. This is disgusting and should be illegal.

The problem is that, at least in Canada, the legislation has been weaponized by LGBTQ activists and irresponsible politicians to ban all psychological counselling and prayer ministry for conversion back to birth gender (only). This left untrained teachers, school counsellors, LGBTQ activists and unprofessional psychologists and doctors free to encourage transition away from birth gender. This was a great victory for the LGBTQ community and their naïve supporters over the silent majority. They are now free to encourage young children in high school to explore gender alternatives and transition away from their birth gender at an age when they are confused, still discovering, and have not matured into their birth gender. Later as adults, about 80 % regret this hasty and badly informed decision and seek conversion back to birth gender. Only now (in Canada} they are trapped because it is illegal to give them the professional psychological counselling and/or prayer ministry they need to transition back to birth gender.

The irresponsible and opportunistic politicians who supported this legislation need to be challenged and replaced by more responsible politicians who will:

1. Revise this legislation to allow only informed adults who have had professional psychological counselling to receive medical assistance,

2. Revise the legislation so anyone can seek professional psychological or spiritual counselling and healing to and from birth gender, and,

3. Protect children in schools from LGBTQ activists, unprofessional teachers, and guidance councillors.

The other part of this is the medical profession's irresponsible and unprofessional participation in sexual conversions. There are criminal investigations ongoing in the United Kingdom against clinics that performed conversion surgery on children. A recent U.K Government review concluded that:

"There is no robust evidence that conversion therapy can change sexual orientation or gender identity, and that conversion therapy is frequently associated with harm."[137]

One can only hope this will force the medical profession's governing bodies to stop pandering to activist bullying on social media and establish serious professional guidelines to at least protect children from their unprincipled butchery. The leadership of the medical associations and governing boards involved badly need to be challenged to provide more responsible and professional leadership.

If enough citizens fail to affirm the seven lost spiritual truths of the foundation, engage with the issues and vote wisely we will all end up living in a failed state. Truth, freedom, and democracy are worth fighting for.

Endnotes

Introduction

1 Calcutt, Clea (October 19, 2021). "French education minister's anti-woke mission". *Politico*. Archived from the original on October 20, 2023. Retrieved November 27, 2022.

2 Morgan, Marcyliena (2020). "'We Don't Play': Black Women's Linguistic Authority Across Race, Class, and Gender". In Alim, H. Samy; Reyes, Angela; Kroskrity, Paul V. (eds.). The Oxford *Handbook of Language and Race*. Oxford University Press. pp. 276–277. doi:10.1093/oxfordhb/9780190845995.013.13. ISBN 978-0-19-084599-5.

3 Romano, Aja (October 9, 2020). "A history of 'wokeness'". *Vox*. Archived from the original on November 21, 2020. Retrieved March 2, 2023.

4 Mirzaei, Abas (September 8, 2019). "Where 'woke' came from and why marketers should think twice before jumping on the social activism bandwagon". *The Conversation*. Archived from the original on March 20, 2023. Retrieved April 8, 2021.

5 Cauley, Kashana (February 2019). "Word: Woke". *The Believer*. No. 123. ISSN 1543-6101. Archived from the original on May 10, 2022.

6 *Merriam-Webster.com Dictionary*, Merriam-Webster, merriam-webster.com/dictionary/postmodern. Accessed 18 Sep. 2024

7 global.oup.com/academic/product/oxford-diction-
    aries-premium-9780191836718?q=oxford%20dic-
    tionaries%20premium&lang=en&cc=us

8 Richard Wolin in *Encyclopædia Britannica* explains
    the writings of pioneering postmodern philoso-
    pher Jean-Francis.

9 Iben Thruaholm, *The Spectator*, August 27, 2005, spec-
tator.co.uk/article/denmarks-spiritual-rearmament-
is-a-lesson-for-the-west/

10 Erin Gretzinger, Maggie Hicks, Christa Dutton
    et. al, *Chronicle of Higher Education*. September
    13, 2024 (Downloaded Sept. 21, 2024) 4

11 R. R. Reno, *Return of the Strong Gods: Nationalism,
    Populism and the Future of the West*, p. 141, Kin-
    dle location 2205.

12 George M. Trevelyan. *England Under the Stewarts.*
    (New York: Methuen & Co., 1980) p. 57.

Chapter 2: Human Reason as False Truth

13 Jordan B. Peterson, *Beyond Order; 12 More Rules for
    Life* (Toronto: Random House Canada, 2023),
    p. 162.

14 Jordan B. Peterson (2023), Ibid.

15 Francis Schaeffer, *How Shall We Then Live?* (Old
    Tappan, N.J.: Fleming H. Revel, 1976), p. 32.

16 Francis Schaeffer, Ibid.

17 Francis Schaeffer, Ibid.

18 Francis Schaeffer, Ibid.

19 Francis Schaeffer, Ibid.

20 Lucy Freeman, *Freud Rediscovered* (Westminster, Maryland: Arbor House, 1980), p. 22.

21 Lucy Freeman, Ibid.

22 Lucy Freeman, Ibid.

23 Daniel Goleman, *Vital Lies, Simple Truths: The Psychology of Self-Deception* (New York: Simon & Schuster, 1985), p.8.

24 Daniel Goleman, Ibid.

25 Francis Schaeffer (1976), Ibid., p. 26.

Chapter 3: Liberalism as False Christianity

26 Francis Schaeffer (1976). Ibid.

Chapter 4: Climate Change as False Science

27 Bjorn Lomborg, *False Alarm: How Climate Change Panic Costs Us Trillions, Hurts the Poor, and Fails To Fix the Planet.* (New York: Basic Books 2020)

28 Bjorn Lomborg, Ibid., p. 6.

29 Stephen Koonin, *Unsettled: What Climate Science Tells, what it Doesn't and Why It Makes a Difference* (Dallas, Texas: Ben Bella Books Inc. 2021 p. 56.

30 Stephen Koonin, Ibid., p. 51.

31 Stephen Koonin, Ibid., p. 88.

32 Stephen Koonin, Ibid., p. 31.

33 Stephen Koonin, Ibid.

34 John R. Christie, Testimony before U.S. House Committee on Science, Space and Technology, March 29, 1917

35 Fritz Varenholt and Sebastian Luning, in a summary of their new book *Unerwunschte Wahrheiten (Unwanted Truth)* (Germany: Clintel.org 12 October 2020). p. 7.

36 Varenholt and Luning, Ibid.

37 `unfecc.int/files/essential_ background /background_publications_htmlpdfapplicatioo/pdf/conveg.pdf`

38 Stephen Koonin (2021), Ibid., p. 65.

39 Guus Berkhout, "There is No Climate Emergency." Letter to Sr. Antonio Guterres, Secretary-General, United Nations.

40 Guus Berkhout, Ibid.

41 Stephen Koonin (2021), Ibid., p. 135.

42 Nigel Lawson, *An Appeal to Reason: A Cool Look at Global Warming* (New York: Duckworth, 2008) p. 50.

43 D. Wingham et. All, "Mass balance of the Antarctic ice sheet". *Philosophical Transactions of the Royal Society*. A, 364, pp. 1627-34.

44 Nigel Lawson (2008), Ibid.

45 Lomborg (2020), Ibid., p. 21.

46 Stephen Koonin (2021), Ibid., p. 134.

47 Stephen Koonin (2021), Ibid., p. 135.

48 Stephen Koonin (2021). Ibid.

49 Bjorn Lomborg (2020), Ibid., p. 69.

50 Bjorn Lomborg (2020), Ibid.

51 Bjorn Lomborg (2020), Ibid.

52 Bjorn Lomborg (2020), Ibid.

53 Bjorn Lomborg (2020), Ibid., p. 155.

54 forbes.com/sites/markpmills/2015/08/07/the-
clean-energy-plan-will-collide-with-the-in-
credibly-weirdphysics-of-the-electric-grid/

55 Rupert Darwell, *Green Tyranny: Exposing the Totalitarian Roots of the Climate Industrial Complex*
(New York: Encounter Books 2017) p. 207.

56 Rupert Darwell, Ibid.

57 Bjorn Lomborg (2020), Ibid., p. 169.

58 Robert Wimmer, (Undated summary of Toyota
Head of Environmental Research); Testifying
before U.S Senate, March 16, 2021.

59 Bjorn Lomborg (2020), Ibid., p. 97.

60 Rupert Darwell (2017), Ibid., p. 147.

61 Rupert Darwell (2017), Ibid., p. 7.

62 Rupert Darwell (2017), Ibid., p. 47.

63 Rupert Darwell (2017), Ibid.

64 Rupert Darwell (2017), Ibid., p. 103.

65 Rupert Darwell (2017), Ibid., p. 138.

66 Rupert Darwell (2017), Ibid., p. 8.

67 Rupert Darwell (2017), Ibid.

68 Rupert Darwell (2017), Ibid., p. 146.

69 Rupert Darwell (2017), Ibid., p. 203.

70 Rupert Darwell (2017), Ibid., p. 219.

71 Rupert Darwell (2017), Ibid., p. 232.

72 en.wikipedia.org/wiki/Climate_change_in_France.
Downloaded September 25, 2023.

Chapter 5: Feminism as False Female

73 John Gishler, *Going Spiritual: Discovering, Developing and Healing a Spiritual Life*, (Calgary: Gishler Group 2018) p. 167.

74 Karl Stern, *The Flight from Women* (St. Paul, Minnesota: Paragon House, 1989 reprint of 1965), p. 15.

75 Karl Stern, Ibid., p. 22.

76 Karl Stern, Ibid., p. 15.

77 Karl Stern, Ibid.

78 Erickson, E H., "Sex differences in the play configurations of preadolescents." *Am. J. Orthopsychiatry.* 21, 667, 1951.

79 Karl Stern (1989), Ibid., p. 9.

80 Karl Stern (1989), Ibid., p. 42.

81 Karl Stern (1989), Ibid.,. p. 56.

82 Karl Stern (1989), Ibid., p. 72.

83 John Gishler (2018), Ibid.

84 `https://www150.statcan.gc.ca/n1/daily-quotidien/220309/dq220309aeng.htm` (downloaded 2022/07/15).

85 `https://www150.statcan.gc.ca/n1/daily-quotidien/220309/dq220309aeng.htm` (downloaded 2022/07/15).

86 Richard Lewis Dougdale, *The Jukes: a Study in Crime, Pauperism, Disease and Heredity* (New York: G.P. Putnam and Sons, 1877.

87 Arthur H. Estabrook, *The Jukes in 1915* (Carnegie Institute of Washington), 1916, p. 1.

disabilitymuseum.org/dhm/lib/detail.html? id=759&page=all. Downloaded Nov. 17, 2022.

88 http:/gutenberg.org/files/15623/15623-h/15623-h.htm

89 David Frum, *What's Right: The New Conservatism and What It Means for Canada.* (Toronto: Random House), 1996, p. 263.

90 Leanne Payne, *Crisis In Masculinity.* (Westchester, Illinois: Crossway Books), 1985, p. 12.

91 Mo Rocca, "The Gay Activists Who Fought the American Psychiatric Establishment," www.lithub.com (Simon and Schuster, November 6, 2017), accessed Nov. 9, 22.

92 Mo Rocca, Ibid.

93 Mo Rocca, Ibid.

94 Mo Rocca, Ibid

95 Jordan Peterson, "The coup of the American Psychological Association is now complete," *National Post*, Feb. 2, 2019, p. A6.

96 Christine Rosen, "The Psychological War on Masculinity," (*Social Commentary*, February 2019, p. 8-9.

97 Christine Rosen, Ibid.

98 Christine Rosen, Ibid.

99 Christine Rosen, Ibid.

100 Christopher West, *Theology of the Body Explained*, Pauline Books and Music, 2003, p. 12., on John Paul II. Homily on the Feast of the Holy Family, December 30, 1988.

101 Derrick Bailey, *Homosexuality and the Western Christian Tradition*, (Shoe-String Press reprint: Hamden Connecticut, 1975, p. 5.

102 Derrick Bailey, Ibid., p. 27.

103 Matthew 5.17.

104 John Gishler (2018), Ibid., p. 166-8.

105 John and Paula Sandford, *The Transformation of the Inner Man*, (South Plainfield, N.J.: Bridge Publishing, 1982), pp.295-317.

106 John and Paula Sandford, Ibid., pp.310.

107 John and Paula Sandford, Ibid., pp.313.

108 Gerald Vanden Aardweg, *Homosexuality and Hope* (Ann Arbour, Michigan. Servant Books, 1985), p. 32.

109 Karl Stern (1989), Ibid., p. 9.

110 Karl Stern, Ibid., p. 12.

111 David C. Geary. *Quillette*, 20 Oct. 2020. (citing Maccoby, E.E. (1990) "Gender and relationships: A developmental account," *American Psychologist*, 45, 513-520.; (1998); *The Two Sexes: Growing up apart, coming together*, Cambridge, MA: Harvard University Press; and Whiting, B. B. & Edwards, C.P. (1988), *Children of different worlds: The formation of social behaviour*.)

112 Leanne Payne (1985), Ibid.

113 Leanne Payne, *The Broken Image: Restoring Personal Wholeness Through Healing Prayer*. (Westchester Illinois: Cornerstone Books, 1981), p. 6.

114 Leanne Payne, Ibid., p. 89.

115 Leanne Payne, Ibid., p. 92.

116 Leanne Payne, Ibid.

117. Leanne Payne, Ibid.

118 Leanne Payne, Ibid, p. 95.

119 Leanne Payne, Ibid.

120 `www.gov.uk/government/publications/an-assessment-of-the-evidence-on-conversion-therapy-for-sexual-orientation-and-gender-identity/an-assessment-of-the-evidence-on-conversion-therapy-for-sexual-orientation-and-gender-identity`. Downloaded 2024-05-10.

121 `cfla-fcab.ca/en/guidelines-and-position-papers/statement-on-intellectual-freedom-and-libraries`, downloaded 2023-01-24.

122 R. R. Russo (1982), Ibid., location 139190.

123 Rene Russo (1982), Ibid., location 139190.

124 Peter L. Levin, *Quillette*, November 2021.

125 John and Mark Sandford, *Deliverance and Inner Healing*, (Grand Rapids: Chosen Books, 2008).

126 Jordan Peterson, *National Post*, March 30, 2024, p. A10

126 Merriam-Webster.com. Retrieved February 6, 2026.

127 Canada, Statutes of Canada. Retrieved January 27, 2026.

128 Leg.gov.uk downloaded February 1, 2026.

129 "Combatting Antisemitism, Hate and Extremism (Criminal and Migration Laws)," Bill 2026. `https://tinyurl.com/5aws5bef` (Retrieved February 6, 2026).

[131] Mirriam-Webster.com retrieved February 14, 2024.

[132] *National Post*, December 28, 2023, Section A8.

133 Francis Schaeffer (1976), Ibid., p. 26.

134 David Frum (1996), Ibid., p. 278.

135 Arthur H. Estabrook (1916), Ibid.

136 David Frum (1996), Ibid., p. 267.

Chapter 6: Homosexuality As False Male

137 www.gov.uk/government/publications/an-assessment-of-the-evidence-on-conversion-therapy-for-sexual-orientation-and-gender-identity/an-assessment-of-the-evidence-on-conversion-therapy-for-sexual-orientation-and-gender-identity, Downloaded 24-05-17.